Song‑Poems
from
Xanadu

Michigan Monographs in Chinese Studies
Volume 64

柯潤璞教授著

上都樂府 續集

受業 彭鏡禧 敬題

Song-Poems *from* Xanadu

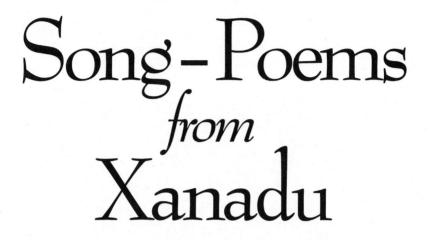

J. I. Crump

Center for Chinese Studies ◆ University of Michigan

Center for Chinese Studies Publications
104 Lane Hall
The University of Michigan
Ann Arbor, Michigan 48109

Cover design: Heidi Dailey
Cover illustration: Edward Trager

Printed on acidfree paper in the United States of America
5 4 3 2 1

Library of Congress Cataloging-in-Publication Data

Crump, J. I. (James Irving), 1921-
Song-poems from Xanadu / by J. I. Crump
   p.   cm.— (Michigan monographs in Chinese studies ; no.
64)
Includes bibliographical references and index.
ISBN 0-89264-094-4 (cloth : alk. paper)
ISBN 0-89264-095-2 (pbk. : alk. paper)
1. San ch'ü —History and criticism. I. Title. II. Series.
PL2354.4.C78 1993
895.1'14209—dc20   92-39788
                                                                CIP

To My Colleagues in the Department

whose companionship, scholarship, and knowledge furnished brains for me to pick while creating this book, and whose patience and generosity provided a home where it could be written, and to Professors Perng Ching-Hsi and S. H. West, erstwhile students and longtime friends: the former read a draft with great skill and care and beautified the final product with his elegant calligraphy; the latter's invitation to speak at Berkeley formed the book's genesis. He later wrote kind words about it while deeply engaged in still other labors on behalf of its author.

Contents

Preface

In Xanadu did Kublai Khan
A stately pleasure dome decree;
Where Alph, the sacred river, ran
Through caverns measureless to man
Down to a sunless sea.

S.T. Coleridge

If the title *Song-Poems from Xanadu* seems hauntingly familiar to the reader, it is because there is another book called *Songs from Xanadu*,[1] written by the same author between 1979 and 1983, primarily as a rigorous attempt to make some sense out of the technical

---

[1] Ann Arbor: Center for Chinese Studies, University of Michigan, 1983. Michigan Monographs in Chinese Studies, no. 47. Hereafter, *Songs*.

and prosodic questions which these songs raise about themselves. The editor at the Center for Chinese Studies noted somewhat wistfully that *Songs from Xanadu* would have been a perfect title for the present book. Since I had already used that title upon a somewhat stuffier work, I tried to mollify him by choosing a title that sounded as much like the one he preferred as possible. Being largely directed at specialists in Chinese literature, the first book differs greatly from this, its sequel, which is written for those who know next to nothing about the subject. The differences between the two publications can be made clear with a single example:

Legend has it that a certain Feng Tzu-chen wrote, on command, forty-two versions of a single song-poem all on one snowy day he spent near Xanadu with a troupe of singing-girls. He also wrote a preface to go with those poetic efforts. In *Songs* I devoted ten pages to the preface and generated thirty-two prosodic graphs from its information, but neither explored the enchanting conditions under which Feng was supposed to have written the songs nor translated any number of them for my readers. The present work rectifies this situation—a whole section is devoted to Feng, translations of his songs, and the circumstances under which they were created (chapter 4). In *Songs* I wrote, "I found several of his forty-two to be as fresh sounding as though they had just sprung to his mind and so particularized that they sound like personal experiences," but in *Song-Poems* I have included translations of a good number of them so readers may judge their quality for themselves. If you would like to understand the prosodic implications of Feng's preface, read *Songs;*

if you know nothing of prosodic questions and would as lief things stayed that way, good; keep the present book on your night-stand.

In short, *Song-Poems from Xanadu* is an attempt to share with the reader my love for the liveliness, breadth of subject matter, and poetic beauty of these songs from Xanadu.

But why Xanadu? The reader needs only three facts to come up with an answer: (1) Among the earliest missionaries to China were Jesuits from Portugal and Spain. (2) If you look at an old Spanish map of Spain, you will find that the town from which English "sherry" (the fortified wine) got its name is spelled *Xeris* (modern *Jeres*). From this you may fairly presume that Spanish speakers once used *x* to transcribe a sound we would write as *sh*. (3) In Chinese, the suffix *du* usually means "capital city." Kublai Khan's summer palace (Coleridge's "stately pleasure dome") was said to be located in the *Shang* (upper) *du* (capital), which Marco Polo writes as *Chandu*. But one of the best-known romanizations for this place, brought back by the Jesuits, perhaps, resulted in "Xanadu"—how that extra *a* managed to insert itself between *Shang* and *du* in Coleridge's "Kublai Khan" is a puzzle. My guess is that it simply sounded more euphonic to his poet's ear.

So, reader, this is a book of song-poems from the Khan's capital—and from many other places in China during the age of Mongol domination—to be appreciated as pieces of literature. I hope you like these English versions as much as I enjoyed translating them.

J. I. C.

Introduction

It appears that sometime toward the end of the Southern Sung dynasty (1127–1279) a new style of music, heavily modal in structure and perhaps already popular among the Jurched tribes of the northeast, was introduced into northern China— probably while that region was ruled by the Chin dynasty (1115–1234)—after which it remained very much the vogue for some six decades. As with musical fads everywhere (the waltz, the tango, jazz, for example) this new form was soon exploited by the entertainment world and became even more widespread. The rhythmic skeletons of these songs later became the frameworks for a favored kind of fixed-form verse (the *san-ch'ü*)—featuring frequent rhyme and irregular line length—to which composers could write their own words.[1] It is believed that

---

[1] There are in extant works some three hundred titles *(ch'ü-p'ai)* of these "song matrices," as they will be called in this book. This somewhat cumbersome designation is needed because we have left to us today only the meters and some formal requirements of what once were musical compositions—the melodies long ago vanished into the dusty air of North China.

throughout most of the life of this form, lyrics written to these song rhythms were sung, either diffidently by the literatus without much musical talent in the privacy of his own study (the fourteenth-century equivalent of our shower-bath baritone), or sung *for* the composer by professional entertainers at banquets and other social occasions. It is certain, however, that with the passage of time, men did compose poetry to these matrices that was only meant to be read, but the resulting verse still retains many musical characteristics: musical nonsense syllables, repeats which make more musical than literary sense, stutter words, reprises, and refrains.

All these compositions (referred to collectively in this book as songs from Xanadu) took one of two major forms—the short lyric *(hsiao-ling)* or the long song-set *(san-t'ao* or *lien-t'ao).* The latter consisted of a number of *hsiao-ling* (related to one another by belonging to the same mode) strung together to form self-contained units. In the musical drama of the age, for example, an act was distinguishable as such when the song-set changed its mode—there was no curtain to descend—the change from one mode to another signaling the end of a song-set and a major dramatic division. In the world away from the stage, the song-set was used by poets for longer narrative pieces and/or fuller, often humorous, treatment of a subject. "In Dispraise of Snow" (chapter 2) is a good example of the latter type. There are several other clever examples of the narrative potential inherent in the *san-t'ao* to be found in *Songs from Xanadu*. I once wrote about the subject matter of songs:

> The Yuan poet was characterized by a willingness to explore far more topical *terra incognita* and do it in a manner less hampered by tradition than ever before; in addition, he had an incomparable arsenal of verse forms with which to invade these territories. . . . The fact that despite these experiments composers largely stuck to a few themes in the majority of their *ch'ü* verse is testimony either to the popularity of the subject matter itself (slightly erotic love songs and the joys of retirement) or to the power of the genre's form and conventions over its subject matter.[2]

Whatever the reason, these two topics statistically outweigh all others for *san-ch'ü* by a wide margin. The *Ch'üan-Yuan San-ch'ü* (Complete Yuan Songs) is the best and most widely used anthology of Yuan songs, incorporating the contents of 117 earlier collections.[3] It contains a set of no less than sixty songs on retirement and seclusion *(kuei-yin)* by a single composer, and the first chapter of the present book, though entirely devoted to various types of love songs, presents the reader with a good deal less than one tenth of 1 percent of the love-song corpus in *CYSC*. This preference in subject matter holds for both the short song and the song-set.

---

[2] *Songs*, p. 10. The reader should keep in mind that songs from Xanadu were earliest and most frequently sung by professionals in various houses of entertainment, where, one suspects, banquets for retiring officials were traditionally held.

[3] Sui Shu-sen, ed. Beijing, 1964; reprint edition, Taipei, 1969. Hereafter referred to as *CYSC*.

This does not mean songs from Xanadu lack variety. On the contrary, I am frequently amazed by the range of topics in what are, after all, supposed to have been simply popular songs. The following little drinking song (done in the carefree persona of a woodcutter) is the kind of thing I would expect most songs daily on the lips of fourteenth-century *mobile vulgus* to resemble:

> We finished the vat to the lees over there,
> We cracked the jug of dregs that was here.
> But now I've peddled my firewood—
> Good!
> The money in my tunic's mine
> To buy us all a round of wine,
> And my gourd is hanging near—
> So gather 'round, friends, and share the cheer.

(Wu Hung-tao. *Chin-tzu Ching*. 727.2)[4]

However, just as often you may come upon pieces which express the most delicate sentiments in subtle and elliptical images:

Singing of What I See

> A young miss in the garden have I seen,
> Perhaps as old as seventeen,
> Watching a pair of butterflies at play—
> A fragrant shoulder
> Slumps against the whitewashed wall,

這家村醪盡。那家醅甕開。賣了肩頭一擔柴。哈。酒錢懷內揣。葫蘆在。大家提去來。

後園中姐兒十六七。見一雙蝴蝶戲。香肩靠粉牆。玉指彈珠淚。喚丫鬟趕開他別處飛。

---

[4] Parenthetical references identify the author, the song matrix, and the page and item number in *CYSC*.

One jade finger wipes away
A tear.
Then I hear her call,
Summoning her serving maid:
"Chase them elsewhere, I can't stand them
    here!"

(Anon. *Ch'ing-chiang Yin.* 1744.3)

While the woodcutter's song is a rollicking
piece, completely straightforward, the real burden
of "Singing of What I See" is only alluded to: the
young woman is nubile and her longings are stirred
by the mating flight of butterflies.

A considerable number of songs are so given
over to formal and musical devices (nonsense sylla-
bles resembling English balladry's *hey-non-nonny*
and the like) that their literary content is very dilute.
Some, however, show considerable complexity and
ambiguity. I still puzzle over the author's cranky
Taoist message in the following, for example:

Fearsome enough the storms of life,
So guard your lips and tongue.
"The Heaven that made a duck's legs short
Yet made the crane's legs long."
Oh Fisher! Oh Woodsman! now
Speak ye less of saints and fools;
Many aid one who's found the Tao,
While the bungler's friends are few.
A saint is always someone else,
The fool is never you.

(Ch'en Ts'ao-an. *Shan-p'o Yang.* 145.5)

風波實怕。唇舌休掛。鶴長鳧短天生下。勸漁家。共樵家。從今莫講賢愚話。得

道多助。失道寡。賢。也在他。愚。也在他。

Emotional impact in the short songs ranges from nil in this blithe confection by Yang Na:

Song of the Flea

Small as he is he can nimbly dance
From a fold in the collar
To the waistband of the pants.
The prick of a lance
Is this creature's bite
And he can elude the keenest sight.
How can you capture a creature who
With a somersault can vanish from view?!

(*Hung Hsiu-hsieh.* 1610.1)

to very considerable in this brief piece, written by Chang Yang-hao as he traveled to take up the post of famine-relief director for Shensi:

I questioned the starvelings met on the way
And talked to refugees seen each day.
"Faithful agent of the king," the townsfolk say.
To myself I laugh a rueful laugh:
What have I done except turn my hair grey?

(*Hsi-ch'un Lai.* 413.3)

However, the majority of songs fall fairly high up in the spectrum—much closer to gay than grey.

This kind of variety and contrast is the result of *CYSC's* eclectic nature. We have to keep in mind what was pointed out above; for about sixty years these song matrices were being used simultaneously by garden-variety entertainers for their trade and by

新。路逢餓殍須親問。道遇流民必細詢。滿城都道好官人。還自哂。只落的白髮滿頭

怎生捺。翻箇觔斗不見了。

小則小偏能走跳。咬一口一似針挑。領兒上走到褲兒腰。眼睜睜拿不住。身材兒

gifted and highly literate men and women for elegant social occasions and, less often, for intimate self-expression. If a twentieth-century editor collected every example spared him through half a millennium by chance or plan, he was bound to produce a very heterogeneous aggregation.

In addition to the diversity of their subject matter, songs from Xanadu contain hundreds of metrical forms and devices that lend the treatment of any subject pleasing animation and variety. It is next to impossible to display consistently in translation the songs' metrical shapes while still preserving a decent regard for poetic values; occasionally, however, it has seemed possible to me to suggest something of both:

Opening My Heart to a Friend

The weeds invade
My garden-plot and field.
I'm a bankrupt in my "inherited trade."
The routes to paradise remain
Very well concealed,
And my cloak is in the pawnshop's keep.
Ah, well,
I'll raise my snailshell cup
Get dead drunk and, groggy, fall asleep
Until first birdsong wakes me up.
Sadness?
Dear friend, I know it not.
Joy?
That's also not my lot.

(T'ang Shih. *Shan-p'o Yang.* 1602.3)[5]

田園荒廢。箕裘陵替。桃源有路難尋覓。典鶉衣。舉螺杯。酕醄醉了囫圇睡。啼鳥一聲驚覺起。悲也。未知。喜也。未知。

雞鳴為利。鴉栖收計。幾曾得覺囫圇睡。使心機。昧神祇。區區造下彌天罪。富

貴一場春夢裏。財。漚泛水。人。泉下鬼。

And again, the same form used for quite different subject matter:

Sigh for the Times

Profit they seek from cock-crow on,
And they scheme till the ravens return to nest.
How many wake from a good night's rest?
First, they ply deceitful tricks,
Then prayers to gull the gods, anon;
And what is worse,
For a tittle's worth of gain
They'll sin against the universe . . .
Spring dreams of fame and wealth are vain!
The money—
Froth not worth the taking.
Those men—
Damned souls in the making.

(Tseng Jui. *Shan-p'o Yang.* 493.2)

The distinctive 1,3;1,3 of the last four lines is the hallmark of the song matrix known by the name of *Shan-p'o Yang.* I have tried to reproduce the rhythm of the last four lines in my translations by stressed beats in English. As the reader can see, even in translations of the *ch'ü,* the form is a member of the class called by Chinese long-short-line verse *(ch'ang-tuan-ch'ü),* and the song *Shan-p'o Yang's* characteristic line-length variation gives it its particular appeal. There are songs, however, totally devoid of

---

[5] The number of base characters (syllables) required in each line is 4,4,7;3,3,7;7;1,3;1,3.

line-length variation—*Yen-erh Lo*, for example, consists simply of four five-syllable lines—while other matrices are exuberant not only in their long and short line alternation but also in their total length. A single song may run to as many as sixteen to eighteen lines of varying length, and many matrices allow or demand a reprise *(yao)*, which usually doubles the size of the composition.

In addition to length of line and song, there are, as was mentioned, a number of other devices to lend formal interest to the songs from Xanadu; the most widely used among them is probably parallel lines. Though every song translated in this book contains one or more pairs of these, they are not always evident in the Englishing. The first four lines of the song below, however, (even in translation) are plainly balanced two and two. The content may not be impressive, but the parallelism is plain:

Spring Thoughts

Gosling yellow,
Those sparse willow fronds'
Mallard green,
Clear ripples of the ponds.
Misty, delicate, timely,
The fecund rains fall.
I leave my door ajar,
For the wine of spring sleep
Is the sweetest drunkenness of all.

(Wang Ho-ch'ing. *Yang-ch'un Ch'ü*. 43.1)

An even more insistent parallelism involving no less than four colors and four riverine features

柳
梢
淡
淡
鵝
黃
染
。
波
面
澄
澄
鴨
綠
添
。
及
時
膏
雨
細
廉
纖
。
門
半
掩
。
春
睡
殢
人
甜
。

黃蘆岸白蘋渡口。綠楊隄紅蓼灘頭。雖無刎頸交。卻有忘機友。點秋江白鷺沙鷗。

傲殺人間萬戶侯。不識字煙波釣叟。

(shorelines, shallows, dikes, and sandbars) can be seen in the following:

The Fisherman

His, the shoreline dense with yellow reed,
The shallows marked by white duckweed,
The dike with its green willow tree,
Red nettles edging sandy bars.
No "friend-to-give-his-life" hath he,
But white egret and sandy gull
Dotting the autumn flood,
Guileless, lend him their company—
Untutored fisher on this misty stream,
You have more cause for self-esteem
Than any tyrant of noble blood.[6]

(Po P'u. *Ch'en-tsui Tung-feng.* 200.2)

In addition to parallel couplets (and sometimes triplets), there are also a number of less-often-seen formal devices—some literary and some presumably musically inspired. As an example of the former, let me describe one of the most bizarre, or at least striking, requirements for fixed-form poetry I know of, East or West. It is used frequently in songs from Xanadu and to good effect. It appears there was once a popular metrical/musical pattern that informed a song called "Remembering the Young

---

[6] The independence and self-sufficiency of fishermen and woodcutters is a favorite theme of the *ch'ü* form; these characters are often endowed with an ineffable nobility and wisdom. See chapter 3, as well as *Songs from Xanadu,* chapter 4.

Prince" *(Yi Wang-sun)*. Gradually, for some reason long forgotten, writing new words to this "tune" began to require that the last two lines be constructed using the phrase "one half X and one half Y"—you substituted your own words for X and Y. Love being such an ambivalent thing—both a joy and a trial, both sweet and bitter—this curious verse convention of "half this" and "half that" was particularly felicitous in dealing with that favored *ch'ü* subject matter. Observe this well-known example:

> Little torment, how I love you,
> How I long for you.
> You lead me on until I worry
> Over everything I do.
> I was deceived completely
> By that little speech you made.
> How you mystify—
> Half of you is simple truth,
> The other half's a lie!

(Kuan Han-ch'ing. *Yi-pan'erh.* 156.4)

And also this next "half and half," which pictures (with great compression and considerable charm) self-esteem and righteous indignation battling with love for the other:

About Love

> Beyond the blue-gauze curtain
> The comings and goings cease.
> He kneels beside the bed
> So eager to make peace—
> "You faithless wretch!

多情多緒小冤家。迋逗得人來憔悴煞。說來的話先瞞過咱。怎知他。一半兒眞實一半兒假。

碧紗窗外靜無人。跪在床前忙要親。罵了箇負心回轉身。雖是話兒嗔。一半兒推辭一半兒肯。

將來書信手拈着。燈下姿姿觀覷了。兩三行字眞帶草。提起來越心焦。一半兒絲

掃一半兒燒。

別來寬褪縷金衣。粉悴煙憔減玉肌。淚點兒只除衫袖知。盼佳期。一半兒才乾一

半兒濕。

It was *you* who turned from *me*!"
(My lips speak angry words
In my distress—
But only half of them mean "no,"
The other half mean "yes.")

(Kuan Han-ch'ing. *Yi-pan'erh*. 156.2)

Here are two others to the same matrix, these by Wang Ho-ch'ing, who is well known for his humor and oblique use of form, as you will see later:

Sentiments

He left her, now she's shed
All gay robes of golden thread.
Melancholy make-up has overlaid
That ever more fine-drawn
Face of jade.
Only her tunic knows how she can cry
When scenes from the good times
Fill her mind's eye—
Half the time its sleeves are wet,
Half the time they're dry.

(42.4)

The letter came,
I slid it out with care,
Took it to the lamplight
Avidly to read it there.
Two or three lines are scribbled here—
But nothing's clear.

Every time I pick it up I vex myself anew.
Half the time I search for hints,
And half the time I stew.

(42.3)

In the latter piece, notice his ironic viewpoint; he there envisions the transcendental sweetnesses of a lover's note being trammeled by such a sublunary shortcoming as illegible handwriting!

Another poetic convention, presumably related to music, is the so-called "thimble phrase" *(ting-chen chü)*. This form of repetition consists of the last line of one verse-unit repeated by the first line of the next (here italicized).

I've cast away all household goods
Save a bamboo fence around a hut of thatch.
Living on the mountain, in the woods,
Content to watch
Red leaves and asters that autumns bring,
I pass my life like *old Shao P'ing.*
Old Shao P'ing, who tended his melon patch.
When idle I harvest mountain teas,
Watch gibbons playing in the trees
And flower-stems dangling from the mouths
    of deer.
My boat is beached *beside Old Ford,*
By Old Ford I patch my raft and gear.
When the sun sinks west I find it good—
Since I've read *Huang-t'ing*
And *Tao-te Ching*—
To tend to my simple livelihood.

(Anon. *Shih-pang Ku.* 1764.1)

把黃庭道德都看罷。別是生涯。

悶採茶芽。閒看青松猿戲耍。樂鹿銜花。舟橫在古渡。古渡整釣槎。夕陽西下。

將家私棄了。向山間林下。竹籬茅舍。看紅葉黃花。待學那邵平。邵平多種瓜。

Some short songs *(hsiao-ling)* are extended by simply repeating the matrix again and again, and a minimal kind of unity for this type of episodic composition is achieved by thimbling the last line of the first unit with the first line of the second. Or again, thimbling may appear linking two different compositions which are traditionally numbered as separate songs but share thimbled lines which unify them as though they were actually two stanzas of the same song:

> Strive for fame who will—
> Fame's a cart careening down the hill
> Whose driver hath no eye
> For pitfalls in its path.
> Today's premier in jadeite halls
> Suffers tomorrow's fatal falls.
> *To hide from wind and waves is best,*
> *Like me in my peaceful, carefree nest.*

(Kuan Yün-shih. *Ch'ing-chiang Yin.* 368.3)

> *Hiding from wind and waves is best*
> *Like me in my peaceful carefree nest.*
> My inside world's immense—
> Sobered up I drink, and then
> Sleep and wake and sleep again—
> Who has more elegant indolence?

(368.4)

By way of at least hitting two birds with one stone, let me compare these examples of the matrix *Ch'ing-chiang Yin* with one other to demonstrate how

競功名有如車下坡。驚險誰參破。昨日玉堂臣。今日遭殘禍。爭如我避風波走在

安樂窩。

似我。避風波走入安樂窩。就裏乾坤大。醒了醉還醒。臥了重還臥。似這般得清閑的誰

different mood and subject-matter can be while still using the same song form:

A Landscape

A myriad green silk strands
On the weeping willow tree
Provoke this idle imagery:
It joins us in the tears we weep for spring.
And perhaps this river might
(As it did the blossom-reddened rain last
    night)
Float away our sorrowing.

(Ch'iao Cho. *Ch'ing-chiang Yin.* 613.2)

The matrix-title *Ch'ing-chiang Yin* should mean something like "Chant of the Ch'ing River," and in earlier times that probably was the title of a single tune that purported to be a song of the boatmen on the Ch'ing river. Gradually other composers began to set their own lyrics to the tune and, of course, its metrical requirements. If the matrix became popular there could be hundreds of compositions sharing the same matrix title. Taking *Ch'ing-chiang Yin* as our example again, there are 158 compositions under that heading in the *CYSC.*

It is reasonably certain that this is the way all songs from Xanadu evolved, for we have extant a few specimens of the original compositions bearing the original *ch'ü-p'ai* in which contents still match title; these are known as *pen-t'i* in Chinese.

Yuan Hao-wen (1190–1257), one of the earliest composers of *ch'ü*, once wrote four pieces to the matrix *Hsi Ch'un-lai.* The last line of each of these

垂楊翠絲千萬縷。惹住閑情緒。和淚送春歸。倩水將愁去。是溪邊落紅昨夜雨。

reads *hsi ch'un-lai* "be joyful, spring is come." Because Yuan lived during the earliest period of the form, it is generally assumed that these pieces are all *pen-t'i:*

Feast of Spring

Cold-plum petals mottled jade.
Their peak is past—
Yet does their perfume last!
Willow twigs have burst their gold
To let their leafy eyes unfold.
Soft springwind eastering
Floods through house and tower—
The apricot is ripe for gathering.
How right to sing
"Be Joyful for the Coming Spring."

(3.1)

In the next example we are even more certain that we are dealing with the composer and the first uses of the matrix:

Dry Lotus Leaves

Green stems bend
Flexing in the wind.
But the lotus leaves are sere.
Some yellow added,
Some fragrance lost
In last night's heavy frost.
How lonesome the river now that Autumn's
    here.

(Liu P'ing-chung. *Kan Ho-yeh.* 12.1)

梅殘玉靨香猶在。柳破金梢眼未開。東風和氣滿樓臺。桃杏折。宜唱喜春來。

乾荷葉。色蒼蒼。老柄風搖蕩。減了清香。越添黃。都因昨夜一場霜。寂寞在秋江上。

Since Liu P'ing-chung is the only person who ever wrote lyrics to *Kan Ho-yeh*, we are tolerably sure he was the composer of that melody as well as its lyrics. He seems to have enjoyed writing to the song matrix he devised, for there are seven versions of it extant. In four of these the words "dry lotus leaves" appear in the first line of the song, but the other three pieces are on completely different subjects. For example:

South Peak stands.
North Peak stands.
But wracks of vapor shroud
The Cave of the Glorious Sunset Cloud—
Not one thing
Left of Nan-Sung's king.
But as before, on Wu-shan Hill
The wineshop banner flutters still.
Two times, it seems,
Men have dreamt their Chiang-nan dreams.[7]

(13.4)

Classified by subject matter, this is verse of a type called *huai-ku* (holding-antiquity-in-one's-breast). We find the composer vaguely comparing *his* migration south of the Yangtze—real or imagined—with the transportation under Emperor Sung

---

[7] Chiang-nan was the last redoubt of Chinese dynasties conquered in the north. This poem is the closest Liu P'ing-chung, who was an adult during the last days of the Chin dynasty and the early years of the Mongol era, came to voicing complaint against the invader in song—for more on this, see chapter 2.

南
高
峰
。
北
高
峰
。
慘
淡
煙
霞
洞
。
宋
高
宗
。
一
場
空
。
吳
山
依
舊
酒
旗
風
。
兩
度
江
南
夢
。

Kao-tsung (1127–1162) of an entire court southward in response to the threat of Chin invasion a half-century or so earlier: these are the two men who dreamed Chiang-nan dreams. This version of *Kan Ho-yeh* obviously has nothing at all to do with the autumn condition of lotus leaves, the topic of the original song; its composer simply liked the form and used it for other subjects that interested him. This is exactly what we think happened with all the songs from Xanadu; a tune became popular and soon entertainers and other composers began writing their own lyrics to it.

Songs from Xanadu made good poetic use of their irregularity of line. Statistically, lines of five and seven syllables are the most frequent, and four- and six-syllable lines are probably the next most common, while lines of three, two, or one syllable are rather rare. Most of the long or narrative songs make heavy use of the seven-character line to relate sequences of events or to create complex descriptive text. Three- and four-beat lines take well to compact imagery. On the face of it, it might seem that six-beat verse would be good for sustained context (perhaps only a little less flexible than the seven-beat), but the internal divisions of a six-beat line are usually 2,2,2, so the resultant rhythm is more staccato than flowing. The most common internal division of the seven-beat line is 4,3, which appears to take well to text with much semantic work to perform. Long, narrative pieces are usually composed to songs that feature frequent seven-beat lines. One song, which in my opinion makes maximum artistic use of the natural shapes of its lines (7,7,7; 5,6; 4,4,4), is given below.

> *Revisiting the Waterfall*
>
> The loom of heaven stops,
> Its new-moon shuttle's done.
> It wove a snow-silk gauze
> And hung it on this wall of stone;
> Translucent fairy-stuff that's spun
> From "strands of rime and rain,"[8]
> Hanging from the sky,
> Spread forever in the sun, yet will not dry.
> Through the traveller's too-thin cloak
> Its brumey breath strikes chill—
> White rainbow sipping from a stream . . .
> Jade dragon plunging down the hill . . .
> Fair-weather snowstorm cascading as a
>   mountain rill.

(Ch'iao Chi. *Shui Hsien-tzu.* 626.1)

The first three seven-beat lines achieve a very complex conceit: the new moon, as a shuttle, has completed its weaving, and the resulting white gauze has been hung from this stone cliff; the cloth the loom of heaven has woven is not of ordinary thread but strands of "rime and rain" that hang

---

[8] The phrase "snow-silk" derives from a story about Shen Yueh in the *Lang-huan Chi.* He meets a nymph with a loom who can weave strands of sleet and rain as others do silk. She presents him with a piece of her wonderful cloth, and he makes a fan of it that cools without even being waved.

天機織罷月梭閒。石壁高垂雪練寒。冰絲帶雨懸霄漢。幾千年曬未乾。露華涼人怯衣單。似白虹飲澗。玉龍下山。晴雪飛灘。

down from the sky.[9] The five- and six-beat lines which follow this *tour de force* top it off with yet another cloth conceit (ordinary material when hung in the sun will dry and bleach, but the miraculous stuff of the waterfall can never change) and then shift attention to the human figure: this serves to introduce the three brilliant four-beat images which form in the traveller's mind. "Revisiting the Waterfall" is highly regarded by Chinese critics; though I have never seen it stated, I believe it is the song's maximum exploitation of various line potentials that, as much as anything, elicits their praise—it certainly does mine.

In addition to the formal flexibilities mentioned so far, there was another large province within which the composer found suppleness and variation. The *ch'ü* form, unlike any other kind of premodern Chinese verse, was exceptionally hospitable to colloquial language. Its ability to combine both literary and vernacular language provides this song form with a pervasive animation impossible to capture in English translations—at least, by this translator. The commonest form for colloquial insertion is the so-called *ch'en-tzu*. These "padding words" usually appear at the head of a line and are disregarded in the requirements for scansion—for which reason they are also called "extra-metrical." We suppose that they were treated as so many light gracenotes when performed, while the verse proper was

---

[9] The image generates poetic power both by its allusive quality and because it reminds the audience that in the natural world "strands of rime and rain" *are* the ultimate source of the waterfall.

嘆貧富十年運。看興亡一著棋。昨朝是今日非。綠草隨春變。青山不改移。白髮

故人稀。恰便似黃葉落東流逝水。

sung with more volume or emphasis. In order to give the reader an approximately congruent sense of their weight, I have italicized the three "padding words" in the following song:

A Sigh for the World

Wealth, alas, waxes or declines
With the circuit of calendric signs.
Calamity, prosperousness—
Results of some cosmic game of chess.
What yesterday believed was right
Will all seem wrong before tonight.
The greenest grass departs with spring—
Black hills alone, unvarying.
My white-haired friends grow fewer by the
     day;
Like so many
Yellowed leaves the river floats away.

(Anon. *Wu Yeh-erh.* 1728.4)

If this introduction to the history and features of songs from Xanadu is to serve its purpose, it should help the reader more fully to appreciate the song-verse found in the rest of the book. It is my hope, however, that the songs will be appealing with or without this background.

1

Songs of Love
and Related Matters

Oh, love, how thou art tired out by rhyme!
Thou art a tree whereon all poets climb
And from thy branches everyone takes some
Of thy sweet fruit which fancy feeds upon.

Lady Margaret Cavendish

Humanity comes in a bewildering number of sizes, colors, and shapes but is the same animal wherever found, and so all societies, ancient and modern, have had to deal (one way or another) with that uniquely human, glorious madness we call in English, "falling in love." How the intensities of this obviously important human pair-bonding phenomenon are handled

風擺簷間馬。
雨打響碧窗紗。
枕剩衾寒沒亂煞。
不著我題名兒罵。
暗想他。
式情
雜。
等來家。
好生的歹鬥咱。
我將那廝臉兒上不抓。
耳輪兒揪罷。
我問你昨
夜宿
誰家。

by societies varies in different eras and places, but to the best of my knowledge, in all human groups (no matter how they have sorted themselves out) members fall in love with one another.

If we observe the amount and intensity of our modern music's preoccupation with love, we can be certain that love, loving, and loving companionship have a great, though somewhat imponderable, importance in our society. The corpus of songs from Xanadu exhibits the same preoccupation—I know of no other poetic form in the history of China which is so devoted to love and sexual attraction in all its aspects.[1]

No matter how far apart in time and space human groups are, it is remarkable how similar all their descriptions of love sound. I doubt you could find two societies more disparate than those of twentieth-century America and fourteenth-century China, but jealousy, for example, is a universal human trait and always a potential part of being in love, so the anonymous Mongol dynasty song below probably rings as true to today's reader as it did in Kublai Khan's capital city when it was first sung.

> Wind disturbing the eave-chimes again.
> Cloth at the window rustles with rain.
> That empty pillow,
> Cold counterpane
> All tangled up with me,

---

[1] Sung dynasty *tz'u* poetry comes closest, but a much smaller percentage concerns itself with what we have been calling love.

I curse with fine particularity.
My emotions are confused and dim
But the darker thoughts are reserved for him!
Oh, wait till he comes back here,
Then won't I pick a fight!
And scratch his face!
And twist his ear!
And where did *you* sleep all last night!?

(*San-fan Yü-Lou-jen.* 1675.2)

Then, as now, there were faithless and exploitive lovers, so there were going to be songs about them. Falling in love demands unqualified attachment—even if only for brief periods of time; exclusiveness is, after all, simply jealousy turned inside out. Such exclusivity and the demand for it are so much a part of our Western love songs that we take its expression for granted.

But if only one of the pair remains in love, he or she becomes extremely vulnerable to exploitation by the beloved. Read this song by Ma Chih-yüan and visualize the situation it supposedly alludes to:

I told you what was in my heart.
"None the less," you said once more,
"It's time we part."
Later, those cruel words
On your oath you swore
Were only said in jest;
Is that supposed to calm
The turmoil in my breast?

(*Shou-yang Ch'ü.* 247.8)

心間事。說與他。動不動早言兩罷。罷字兒磣可可你道是耍。我心裏怕那不怕。

輕拈斑管書心事。細摺銀箋寫恨詞。可憐不慣害相思。則被你個肯字兒。迤逗我許多時。

And in the next piece the burden is the same, only the words are different:

On Love

Her dappled brush with failing fingers
    gripped,
She tries to tell the feeling in her breast.
On silvered sheets, fine-folded,
She writes this anguished script:
"Alas, till now I've never been oppressed
By a faithless lover's wrong—
'I will, I will,' you did protest,
And led me on for—oh, so long."

(Po P'u. Yang-ch'un Ch'ü. 195.1)

Was there ever a literate society in which similar plaintive notes from jilted or abandoned lovers can't be found?

The same question may be asked of what we call lovesickness. The "Song of Songs" says "Stay me with flagons, comfort me with apples; for I am sick of love." The *New Jerusalem Bible* uses a more modern idiom, "sick with love," and cites Second Samuel (13:2): "Amnon the son of David loved Tamar and Amnon was so vexed that he fell sick for Tamar." It goes on to note that these are the only uses of the term *lovesick* in the Bible, but that it is often to be found in nearly contemporary Egyptian songs.[2] Millenia later Giles Fletcher's

---

[2] P. 1033, note c.

"Wooing Song" from the seventeenth century sounds the same theme:

> Love no med'cine can appease,
> He burns the fishes in the seas:
> Not all the skill his wounds can stench,
> Not all the sea his fire can quench.

Fiction and poetry in China abound with the lover deprived of his or her love: listless, losing weight, sighing gustily, lackluster of eye—all the symptoms known worldwide. We, today, generally treat the malady with sympathy and patience, knowing that it is real enough, but rather easily cured. The Chinese likewise:

On Love

> Love's grip on the marrow of the bone
> No knife, no drench can mitigate;
> It's a morbid illness of the Vital Zone[3]
> No treatment will alleviate:
> There are no remissions for the yearning heart!
> Yet the symptoms vanish without a trace
> When you and I are face to face.

(Wang Ho-ch'ing. *Hsi Ch'un-lai.* 43.2)

My second lovesick song-poem happens to be from two sets of four addressed to the same person. I shall treat that whole intriguing group below under

---

[3] *Kao-huang:* cf. our "solar plexus."

情粘骨髓難揩洗。病在膏盲怎療治。相思何日會佳期。我共你。相見一般醫。

今日裏不如死。 | 從他嫁了時。情懷兩不知。終日病相思。如醉復如癡。鱗鴻雖有難投字。思知。 | 情如醉。悶似癡。春瘦怯春衣。添憔悴。廢寢食。減腰肢。怎脫厭厭病體。

another heading but I want to here include one as an example of lovesickness symptoms which echoes so much that is familiar in Western counterparts:

> Besotted by love,
> By melancholy made lack-wit:
> Spring emaciation shamed
> By spring robes' fit.
> Less nightly sleep, less daily bread—
> More haggard, more spindling;
> Trunk and limbs dwindling . . .
> Oh, would this hateful body could be shed!

(Lo Chih-an. *Wu Yeh-erh.* 1128.3)

Note that "spring emaciation" above refers not just to the season but to lovesickness itself, just as it does in the songs written by Liu Chih to burlesque his friend the Tutor's infatuation with beauteous Mistress Spring (see below).

And finally, this song of lovesickness by Ching Yuan-ch'i:

Lovesick Young Woman

> Ever since the day he wed,
> He's shown me no tenderness or heart.
> I'm lovesick every day that we're apart,
> Like being drunk with all my senses numb.
> Though I had a willing goose or fish
> My notes would lie unread—
> I know he knows
> Today I wish that I were dead.[4]

(*Te-sheng Ling.* 1149.1)

(The carp and the goose, by reason of historical and poetic allusions, are frequently the bearers of notes between lovers, as you will see below in the section devoted to "Emotions in the Women's Quarters.")

One personage, however, was explicitly excluded from the generally lighthearted view of the excesses often accompanying the state of "being in love." Chinese society recognized love to be a benign form of madness, and was reluctant to have its ruler (with his absolute power) in the throes of any madness, no matter how benignant. Note the gravity of this song-poem from Xanadu by T'ang Shih called "The Concubine T'ai-chen," better known to us as Yang Kuei-fei:

> So besotted was the emperor
> Of the era called K'ai-yuan,
> With lust for love and luxury, that when
> He took Kuei-fei to wife,
> The Eastwind blew to fecundate
> New-greened sprouts of strife.
> A mother still hoped with bated breath,
> But her plump girl-child was doomed to death.
>
> *(yao)*
> Fated to end were omens of peace;
> The alarm of Tatar pipes in Yü-yang echoing,

開元天子好奢華。眞妃選作渾家。東風吹動禍根芽。娘牽掛。沒亂煞胖娃娃。

不隄防變卻承平卦。鬧漁陽一片胡笳。辭鳳榻。遷鸞駕。馬嵬坡下。踏碎海棠花。

---

[4] This, however, is a strangely ambiguous song. The title could also be translated "Yearning for My Mistress," but the verb, "to wed," is one used of women. However, if the "I" in this song is a man, it would be the only example of a lovesick male in this rather considerable sub-genre.

To Ma-wei slope they dragged her from the
Phoenix Bed,
Tied to the chariot of her king.
And there a trampled hibiscus now lies dead.

(*Hsiao Liang-chou.* 1575.2)

Notice that the act of taking Yang Kuei-fei to wife
caused, in some transcendental fashion, the "sprouts
of calamity" to flourish, and, in the reprise *(yao)*, the
omens of peace for which the emperor's reign had
theretofore been noted were fated to end because of
his infatuation with her.

I know of no similar song from Xanadu which
celebrates the other fabled imperial indiscretion—
one which is even more apposite since it involved
the famous Southern Sung courtesan Li Shih-shih:
whatever her shortcomings, Yang Kuei-fei was not,
after all, a singing-girl. That I cannot find in Yuan
songs poetic elaboration of the emperor Hui-tsung's
infatuation with the famous "entertainer" is prob-
ably because only a century and a half had elapsed
between the time this affair supposedly occurred
and the beginning of the period (approximately A.D.
1280–1340) when most of our songs from Xanadu
were written. Legend-building takes time, and this
liaison became best known through the curious his-
torico-fictional pastiche known as *Hsüan-ho Yi-shih*
(Unofficial History of the Hsüan-ho Reign)[5] which

---

[5] See William O. Hennessey, trans., *Proclaiming Harmony*, Ann
Arbor: Center for Chinese Studies, University of Michigan,
1981. Michigan Monographs in Chinese Studies, no. 41.

was probably being compiled at just the time songs from Xanadu were becoming popular. In this quasi-romance we find the emperor urged by wicked ministers to make nocturnal visits incognito to the marketplace (an ancient folk-tale motif). There he becomes infatuated with the fabled Li Shih-shih and eventually raises her to the imperial harem—over the strong objections of his saintly advisor Chang T'ien-chüeh. Shortly after her elevation, Hui-tsung is taken on a dreamlike flight to the Moon Palace by his pet Taoist adept. There he sees two men, "one dressed in red and the other in black, sitting to the south and north of each other." They explain that they have been ordered by the Celestial Emperor to play chess for rulership of the empire. The one in black wins and departs, laughing, for the north. Hui-tsung realizes that the one in red represents himself and that he is destined to lose his land. He tells Li Shih-shih his dream. She minimizes its importance, but the reader knows that royal infatuation with a courtesan is the straw that is to break the back of Hui-tsung's (and China's) celestial fortunes.

Hui-tsung's affair with a courtesan was improper only because he was emperor. In love songs from Xanadu, the emotions expressed are completely comprehensible to Westerners, but since romantic love in traditional China was for the most part confined to a courtesan context, its social aspects will appear strange at times. Traditional Chinese society, unlike our present one, never believed romantic love could or should be the basis for marriage and family. The overwhelming majority of love songs from Xanadu were written to or about courtesans and their patrons,

for this was the way in which the Chinese tradition-
ally chose to institutionalize and make manageable
"falling in love."

As befits something as complex as romantic
love, the customary Chinese system of bringing to-
gether men and women who were in love was wildly
complicated, being a cross between a geisha system,
a procurer's establishment, and a form of sophisti-
cated public entertainment. While every house-of-
joy was capable of furnishing its clients with
feminine companionship of the most basic sort, what
distinguished the elegant house, one that attracted
literary lions and high officials, from the mere
brothel was the musical talent and education of its
young ladies. The most fashionable houses boasted
skilled and literate (indeed, sometimes literary)
women who composed and sang their own verse,
and it was a matter of social *cachet* for a man to write
songs which might become part of the repertoire of
a well-known courtesan.

The circumstances surrounding the composi-
tion of the following very polished piece, done im-
promptu at a party (we are told), demonstrate the
level of talent found in the best courtesan estab-
lishments. A certain Commander Ting was enter-
taining two eminent writers at the Chiang-hsiang
Gardens, and Wang Yi-fen'erh, "an actress from the
capital whose singing and dancing were matchless
and whose quickness of wit was without peer," was
attending to their cups. One of the younger enter-
tainers sang a song, and Ting noted that the opening
lines had the same rhythm required for the tune
matrix *Ch'en-tsui Tung-feng* and challenged Miss
Wang to complete an original *Ch'en-tsui Tung-feng*

incorporating the song's words, from "Falling leaves" to "some strange snake." He had hardly finished speaking when she sang the song given below, much to the admiration of all present.

> "Falling leaves of autumn red—
> Scales the Fire-Dragon shed;
> Forked top of an old, dead pine—
> Bared fangs of some strange snake."
> Splendid themes for songs to take,
> They might be used
> For paintings, too.
> The guests are happy that
> The count of cups became confused
> Since everyone had changed his mat.
> It's been a dream of Dalasun brew
> Passing in rounds beyond all count.
> But, until I'm much more drunk
> Don't help me to my mount.

(1409.1)

The talented Miss Wang uses the required lines (admittedly in a somewhat perfunctory fashion), shifts the subject to the ambience of the moment, and skillfully "patches in" *(yin-k'uo)* two well-known lines (8–10) by Ou-yang Hsiu. It was just this sort of literary-musical ingenuity that was most highly prized by the *beau monde* of the day.

Love affairs with courtesans had the sanction of the highest levels of urban and court society, either tacit or explicit (with the important exception of the emperor, as we have noted). These arrangements sound (and indeed were) quite commercial, but there

紅葉落火龍褪甲。青松枯怪蟒張牙。可詠題。堪描畫。喜觥籌席上交雜。答剌蘇頻斟入禮廝麻。不醉呵休扶上馬。

從
來
好
事
天
生
儉
。
自
古
瓜
兒
苦
後
甜
。
妳
娘
催
逼
緊
拘
鉗
。
甚
是
嚴
。
越
間
阻
越
情
忺
。

still were many ways within the system for a man
and a woman to establish an exclusive liaison, and
in both fact and fiction there are numerous examples
of courtesans who became legitimate wives (or,
more often, legitimate "secondary" wives) of men of
high social standing. However, my interest is not
sociological, it is to give you glimpses of the situ-
ations and emotions involved in being in love in the
Mongol era, as expressed in the popular songs of
that day, so that you may appreciate how strikingly
similar the responses of thirteenth-century China
were *(mutatis mutandis)* to those of today.

The courtesan and patron system had become
disorganized by the end of Imperial China, and,
unsatisfactory as it was, nothing more workable has
since taken its place. People born after the turn of
this century tend to forget how the older system
operated—to such an extent that it appears several
modern Chinese commentators dealing with the lit-
tle song below mistake the "Mama" in the lyrics for
the biological mother *(mu-ch'in)* of the girl.

Emotions

Lovers thrive on adversity.
"The more bitter the melon at first,
The sweeter the ripe one will be."
Mama pressures, interferes,
Finds stern reasons for delay;
But the more she obstructs,
The happier they!

(Po P'u. *Hsi-ch'un Lai.* 195.4)

Nai-niang, the term used in the song for the woman keeping the lovers apart, is the madam of the house-of-joy, to whom the girl is practically indentured; in the song, Madam is causing trouble over the price and/or conditions the young man must meet for the lady's exclusive attentions.

The built-in weaknesses and contradictions plaguing Chinese conventions of romantic love involving courtesans arise from the commercial aspect and the sharing of the loved one with others. These by their very nature are antagonistic to the exclusivity romantic love demands. The system's shortcomings were just as obvious to the Chinese and the Chinese poet as they are to us. Consider the following by Lu Chih. The song is titled by the composer, "Parting from the Courtesan, Chu-lien Hsiu [Pearl-Screen Elegance]":[6]

> Scarce had we our pleasure taken
> Than we did part.
> Deep, deep the hurt
> To be thus forsaken.
> That pleasure-boat, departing,
> Bears off all my spring.
> Leaving me—worthless now—
> Half a moonlit river, shimmering.

> (*Lo Mei-feng.* 131.4)

才歡悅。早間別。痛煞煞好難割捨。畫船兒載將春去也。空留下半江明月。

---

[6] A gifted actress and composer in her own right (see *CYSC*, pp. 354–55) to whom Feng Tzu-chen is supposed to have indited a song to the matrix *Che-ku T'ien.* See chapter 4.

Before you draw too many heart-rending con-
clusions from this brief piece, however, I hasten to
point out that there are also, in the *CYSC*, other songs
to and about that same intriguing Pearl-Screen Ele-
gance, composed by Hu Ch'i-yü (69.3) and Kuan
Han-ch'ing (170.1), both of whom were probably
friends of, or at least known to, the author of the song
above. I think there must have been a special level
of relationship possible, and perhaps common,
among fellow patrons of the same courtesan—par-
ticularly if she were a famous entertainer whose
clients vied with one another to furnish song lyrics
for her to sing perhaps more often than they did for
her more intimate favors. If someone as well-known
in the *beau monde* as Pearl-Screen Elegance sang the
words you composed for her, it lent you consider-
able social *éclat*. In cases like these we are not really
dealing with romantic love, but with stylish games
involving the two sexes, as played by members of
China's highest social strata.

The next two moderately satirical songs, along
with their preface, demonstrate one way in which
this social game was played. The composer was
merely being clever and teasing a friend for his
infatuation with a singing-girl by composing verses
full of double entendres and puns. Nevertheless, the
three units below reveal a great deal about the social
play that was a part of the system. But, as is often the
case, one learns more only to find more questions
generated by the knowledge.

[Composer's preface:] K'uei Ch'un-ch'ing [Mis-
tress of Spring], the singing-girl from Wu-ch'ang,
was acknowledged to be the most beautiful and

(Collection of the National Palace Museum, Taiwan, Republic of China)

春　春
不　來
許　苦
。　欲
問　伴
春　春
無　居
語　。
。　日
春　日
意　尋
定　春
何　去
如　。
。　無
　　奈
　　春
　　雲
　　不
　　為
　　雨
　　。
　　為
　　春
　　瘦
　　。
　　綠
　　窗
　　誰
　　唱
　　留
　　春
　　住
　　。
　　買

talented entertainer of the time. My friend Wen Tzu-fang, Secretary of the Board of Justice, visited Wu-ch'ang. On this occasion the Tutor An Tzu-chu met K'uei Ch'un-ch'ing and was so taken with her he could not put her out of his mind. I wrote these songs [in his persona] and gave them to him.

I would be Spring's companion every day,
So daily I pursued this Spring.
But lo, her clouds no rain would bring,
So this year Spring has made me waste away.
Outside the window do I not sing
"Forever Let Spring Stay?"[7]
But, alas, Spring can't be bought;
Spring, questioned, always answers naught.
Who can know the mind of Spring?

(Liu Shih-chung. *Hsiao-t'ao Hung.* 659.3)

Spring alone can bring
Cures for the ravages of Spring.
When Spring comes I hope I'm there
Her drunkenness to share—
Even more I long to share Spring's sleeps
But hate the tardy times she keeps.
When I heard that Spring had come last night,
My spring-heart swelled with mute delight,

---

[7] This sounds like a *ch'ü p'ai* (matrix title), but it appears in none of the well-known lists.

Expressing its feeling by the secret gifts I
    bring—
Still, who knows what will happen in the
    spring but Spring?

             (*Hsiao-t'ao Hung.* 660.1)

It is doubtful that these songs were composed
for performance by the beauteous Mistress Spring,
but they were certainly to be performed at some sort
of informal social event. (Anyone who deals with
Yuan dynasty song-poetry must constantly keep in
mind that it was originally designed to be sung,
well or badly, by the poet or someone else.) Notice
that Mistress Spring was free to deny her personal
favors if she wished—"But lo, her clouds no rain
would bring" and "But alas, Spring can't be
bought."[8] And in the second song, "Even more I long
to share Spring's sleeps, / But hate the tardy times
she keeps." The two songs' allusive language has a
long history in the vocabulary of Chinese poetry.
(Few things are praised more often than long sleeps
in the spring, "spring fever," and spring drunken-
ness. The conceit of spring arriving all in one night
can be found in verse from T'ang through Ming.)
However, there can be no doubt that the composer's
primary purpose in writing these verses was to twit
his friend the Tutor for his failure to gain the per-
sonal services of Mistress Spring. Poor Wen Tzu-
fang was only a *chu-chiao*—a post somewhat less

---

[8] The question then presents itself, How much autonomy did
Spring have in such a situation? Or was she herself the madam?

為春憔悴要春醫。苦苦貪春睡。盼得春來共春醉。恨春遲。夜來得箇春消息。春心暗喜。春情偷寄。春事只春知。春

訃音至傷心萬端。挽歌成離恨千般。蝶愁花事空。鳳泣蕭聲斷。麗春園長夜漫漫。

懊恨閻羅量不寬。偏怎教可意嬌娥命短。

lofty than Assistant Professor—and Spring's madam, or Spring herself, was probably well aware that even in those days there wasn't much money to be gotten from academic types.

I don't wish to leave any mistakenly cynical impression now or later: sharing pleasure with a beloved is certainly one of the great sources of deep emotion available to human beings. It is hardly strange, then, that many courtesan liaisons resulted in tender and lasting love affairs. There is oblique evidence for this in a set of songs by T'ang Shih (a late Yuan composer) called simply "Elegies to a Singing-Girl." He obviously had been sent formal notice of her death (the term he uses is *fu-yin*), probably attended her obsequies, and was moved to write four pieces in her honor. It makes one wonder just what relationships were involved here. The first of the set is the most informative:

> Death Notice: stabbing my heart in a
>   thousand ways.
> Funeral Song: reviving grief of a hundred
>   parting-days.
> Butterflies grieve; flowers now serve in vain.
> The Phoenix weeps; the pipes have halted
>   their refrain.
> Nights are long and lonely now in Li-ch'un
>   Yuan.[9]
> I hate thee unforgiving Yama, King of Hell,
> Who sent death so untimely
> To the nymph I loved so well.

> (*Ch'en-tsui Tung-feng.* 1580.3)

The grieving butterflies, weeping phoenixes, and silent pipes are all clichés, but there is something quite moving about the openness and elegiac formality of these four *ch'ü* (a poetic form usually reserved for parties and other lively occasions).

In order that the somewhat sardonic burden of the next songs should be made clear, I must first relate a story. In the Sung dynasty a popular theme for all kinds of fiction and performance literature was the tale (original now lost) of the lovely courtesan Su Ch'ing and her well-born lover Shuang Chien.[10] It was the Sung dynasty equivalent of our Romeo and Juliet and had as many recensions as its Western counterpart. So popular was this love story by the time of the Yuan dynasty that the names of the lovers had become clichés on the lips of everyone—song-writers included. Su Ch'ing and Shuang Chien became standard allusions to all lovers yearning for the absent one.[11] The next piece is an illustration. It is about a lonely beauty yearning for her lover—her lovelorn condition is identified by giving her the name of the heroine and him the name of the hero of that famous love story:

---

[9] A famous house-of-joy.

[10] There is no extant Yuan drama that tells the story, which appears to have been supplanted in popularity during Yuan times by "The Story of Ying-ying." Su Ch'ing and Shuang Chien and the songs they inspired are the subject of chapter 7 of *Songs from Xanadu*

[11] See CYSC 1734.4: "Pity the Su Ch'ing who can't recognize her Shuang Chien"—that is, she doesn't know Mr. Right.

裝呵把長吁來應。推眼疼把珠淚掩。佯咳嗽口兒裏作念。將他諱名兒再三不住的咶。思量煞小卿也。雙漸。

Pretended yawns conceal deep sighs.
To hide her tears she counterfeits sore eyes.
She feigns coughs to help disguise
Complaints that rise
Unbidden to her lips.
His secret name sounds in her murmuring,
Over and over again—
Oh, how our Su Ch'ing longs for her Shuang
        Chien!

(Anon. *Lo-mei Feng*. 1748.2)

The original love story (if there was an actual written original) could have been a musical drama or a narrative medley of songs. In either event, the "original" is lost in the mists of time; the scenario I will now give you is a patchwork job from extant Yuan and Ming productions:

At great expense, Shuang Chien sets Su Ch'ing up in a private menage of her own in the courtyard of the house-of-joy, and they share an idyll. Soon, however, he must return home to get more money to support his love in the custom demanded by the madam. While he's gone, Mama is offered a great deal more money for Su Ch'ing by the villain, a rich tea-merchant named Feng K'uei. In some versions there must also have been a wealthy friend (?) of the tea-merchant called Huang Chao. His part in the mise-en-scène is now unclear.[12] Su Ch'ing is tricked

---

[12] The hints about Huang Chao in Yuan songs are as intriguing as they are inconclusive. For example: "Feng K'uei was as rich / As Shuang Chien was poor. / While the two of them fought

into boarding the tea-merchant's boat, and he bears her triumphantly away to Yü-chang. Shuang Chien makes, or inherits, his fortune, returns to Su Ch'ing; she is gone, but he tracks her down. Eventually he finds the tea-merchant's boat at Yü-chang and takes her back.[13] The next songs allude to characters from this widely known tale, who are used by the composers to poke fun at courtesans, their establishments, and the inevitable commercial considerations that contrast so badly with the demands of romantic love. The title of the first (supposedly given it by the composer Tseng Jui) is "Mocking the Singing-Girl" *(Ch'ao Chi-chia).*

Feng K'uei's rude,
Huang Chao's crude,
But they're both as wealthy as the gods!
It's not that I don't love dear Shuang Chien;
But since madam is tough
And her manner is rough,
It's the money you've got that makes the odds.

(*Ssu-k'uai yü.* 476.1)

---

to be her paramour / (Since one of them was acting like a lump of butter / And the other was burdened by a ton of tea), / Huang Chao most expediently / Stirred up trouble and uncertainty" (Lan Ch'u-fang. *Ssu-k'uai Yü.* 1622.2).

[13] In one version he locates Feng K'uei's boat by hearing her singing. This account is also the basis of acts 2 and 3 of the Yuan drama featuring Po Chü-yi called *Ch'ing-shan Lei (Yuan-ch'ü Hsuan, no. 51).* For comparisons, see Cyril Birch, ed., *Studies in Chinese Literary Genres* (Berkeley: University of California Press, 1974), p. 250.

黃肇村。馮魁蠢。雖有通神鈔和銀。奴非不愛雙生俊。李老嚴。坡撒狠。錢上緊。

There are other songs from Xanadu in which some composer or another ruefully alludes to the disparity between love's young dream and the market realities. Indeed, there is yet another by the composer of 476.1 above which includes the lines:

What's needed is a bit of wealth
To restore lovesick Shuang Chien to health . . .
Tight shut are doors to palaces of pleasure,
But their guardians smile at the sight of
    treasure.

(488.3)

無錢難解雙生悶　．
．粉營花寨緊關門　．
．披撒見錢親　。

Finally, there is the famous full-fledged parody of the story of Su Ch'ing (here called Su-niang) and Shuang Chien by the irreverent Wang Ho-ch'ing. He titles the song "Fat Couple" and composes, with compact and mordant satire, his own version, featuring a corpulent Romeo and an obese Juliet:

A rather obese Master Shuang
Bore off an overweight Miss Su-niang
(Each one of that pair
Was the size of a bear!)
On the wings of romance, off they sped,
But paused a while at Yü-chang to pant—
These lovebirds the size of an elephant—
And bang their bellyskins in bed!

(*Po Pu-tuan.* 47.2)

對兒鴛鴦象　。交肚皮廝撞　。

一箇胖雙郎　。就了箇胖蘇娘　。兩口兒便似熊模樣　。成就了風流喘豫章　。繡幃中一

There is another large subgenre of songs, closely related to those which call themselves something like "on love" or "about love"—the so-called *kuei-*

ch'ing or *kuei-yuan*, "resentment (or emotions) in the women's quarters," where the composer, in the persona of a lonely woman, can summon up langorous love scenes of the past or dwell upon yearning for the departed lover in the present. Most of the time these pieces presuppose that the gentleman has succeeded in removing his loved one from the house-of-joy and installing her in his own women's quarters—only to be called away for any number of reasons, leaving her pining. The following is a good example of the type: it bears no title but is obviously a *kuei-yuan* piece, with its seasonal shift from summer to fall implying the passing of youth and chances for loving congress. This is made explicit, of course, by the unshared bed:

> Fall comes on;
> Bit by bit I feel
> The chill increase.
> Cold from the north
> Migrant geese southward wheel.
> The *wu-t'ung* tree—
> Its yellowing leaf
> Deepening my lonely grief.
> My embroidered spread
> Throughout the night
> Lies undisturbed on half the bed.

(Anon. *Wu Yeh-erh.* 1723.4)

Not all songs of "resentment in the women's quarters" include references to seasonal change, but a great many do—sometimes simply by allusion to the condition of certain flowers. Plum-blossoms

秋
來
到
。
漸
漸
涼
。
寒
雁
兒
往
南
翔
。
梧
桐
樹
。
葉
又
黃
。
好
淒
涼
。
繡
被
兒
空
閒
了
半
張
。

簪
玉
折
。
菱
花
缺
。
舊
恨
新
愁
亂
山
疊
。
思
君
凝
望
臨
臺
榭
。
魚
雁
無
。
音
信
絕
。
何
處
也
。

imply spring, chrysanthemums, fall, and several special summer blooms can set the stage. The next song is a clever double entendre; if the objects in the first two lines are taken as flowers, the scene takes place very late in the summer with the first signs of fall (the tattered condition of the flowers) lending intensity to the woman's worries about lack of news. If the objects are seen as a hair ornament and a mirror respectively (perfectly possible by poetic convention) the lonely lady's listless inattention to her toilette has broken her hairpin, and the broken mirror alludes to separated lovers. I've chosen to translate the flower allusion because traditionally officials stationed far from home would return in the fall to leave their summer garments for repair and pick up winter garb, or send servants to perform the task. Their families' anxiety mounts when the absent one has not returned by autumn. Note that the goose and the carp are mail-carriers again:

> The tuberose has snapped in two.
> All the water-chestnuts' blooms are through.
> Old resentments, recent wrongs,
> Loom as huddled mountains do.
> Like one blind,
> Staring at the kiosk on the garden lawn,
> I think of you.
> No geese, no fish to carry word;
> No news of you has yet been heard—
> Where art thou gone?

> (Tseng Jui. *Ssu-k'uai yü.* 474.2)

橫　千
空　點
幾　萬
行　點
塞　老
鴻　樹
高　寒
　。　鴉
茂　。
林　三
千　行
點　兩
昏　行
鴉　寫
噪　高
　。　寒
　　呀
　　呀
　　雁
　　落
　　平
　　沙
　　。

The southward migration of geese of several
kinds signaled autumn and the period of decline and
decay, just as it does to those of us in the West who
live in the northern temperate zone. Furthermore,
the flocking of crows and ravens in trees—which are
usually beginning to lose their leaves—also marks
(as it does for us) the autumnal season. Given the
frequent demand in Chinese fixed-form poetry for
parallel verse, the two migrants are often found
balancing each other in successive lines.

> Several lines of geese from the border forts
> Slant across the sky.
> In the thick woods a thousand black dots
> Caw their raven cry . . .

(Cheng Kuang-tzu. *Chu-ma T'ing.* 465.1)

And in a song matrix which demands a more com-
plex set of couplets, e.g., *Che-kuei ling*, another and
more elaborate pairing of the two birds to symbolize
autumn can be found:

> A thousand, ten thousand dots of crows
> Settle in the old dead tree.
> Two lines, three lines written across the sky;
> Geese drop to the sandbar in gabbling
>   company.

(Cheng Kuang-tzu. *Che-kuei Ling.* 463.3)

Often the fall goose is joined by crickets seek-
ing warmer niches to pass the winter; in them,
they become more audible to the lonely lady at this
season:

Emotions in the Women's Quarters

The lone goose calls sadly,
Crickets of the cold weep.
While she dreamt, they were not apart;
But now she's startled from her sleep
And sounds from these creatures of loneliness
Have shattered her aching heart.
Blue-black brows knit and grieve,
Little tear-pearls, falling,
Wet her sleeve.

(Tseng Jui. *Ssu-k'uai Yü.* 473.1)

There are a few of these "emotions in the women's quarters," however, in which the lonely woman explicitly calls herself the man's wife—as in the following rather witty song by Hsü Tsai-ssu:

Alas, for the wife of a travelling man!
For I was matched by unkind fate
With a cruel and faithless mate.
"I'm only going to Eastern Wu,"
He told me when he went
These three long years ago.
Now what's to do?
Here's a letter he just sent
By a man from far Kuangchou.

(*Hsi Ch'un-lai.* 1041.3)

You must understand that this particular women's quarters is probably supposed to be located in Hangchou, so that when her travelling man told her he

孤雁悲。寒蛩泣。恰待團圓夢驚回。凄涼物感愁心碎。翠黛顰。珠淚滴。衫袖濕。

妾身悔作商人婦。妾命當逢薄倖夫。別時只說到東吳。三載餘。卻得廣州書。

was going to Eastern Wu, it was someplace about as far as Chicago is from Ann Arbor; suddenly she's gotten a letter postmarked (as it were) Los Angeles.

While the vast majority of love songs from Xanadu concern courtesans, or former courtesans, there are apparent exceptions, and the remainder of this chapter is devoted to these. Unlike the love songs we have described and translated so far, the following songs, which concern lovers' trysts, should probably (though not certainly in all cases) be read as meetings between young men and marriageable young women not in the entertainment trade. Obviously, the songs are so written because such meetings, being forbidden, heightened the literary suspense and risk which is the essence of a tryst; but I have no doubt at all that such encounters were social facts as well—for all the determined chaperoning furnished young women of good families in China!

If vying with one's peers to write love songs for famous courtesans is typical of Chinese rather than of all human beings in love, surely the lover's tryst— with its anxieties, its nervous expectations—is truly universal. The sad tryst of Pyramus and Thisbe at the mulberry tree by Ninus's tomb can glory in a certain antiquity, since Ovid sets the scene in ancient Babylon; but there are few trysting lovers in literature who can antedate these in the *Shih Ching (Book of Songs)*, circa 1000 B.C.:

> Oh, Chung-tzu
> Do not leap the hedgerow to our farm,
> Nor break the willows planted there!
> If the willow suffered harm

I would not care;
It's mother and father that I fear.
Chung-tzu, I do hold you dear,
But the words of my parents I do fear.[14]

Liu T'ing-hsin's song from Xanadu called "Keeping the Tryst" is somewhat trite but calls to mind many others of its ilk to be found East or West.

> All is silent in the deep of night—
> Clear moon shining at its height.
> To the little study no one comes;
> But the student himself is not abed,
> For, whispering to his love he said:
> "No need to tap on your window screen.
> I'll shake the branches of the blossoming tree.
> Remember now—
> Wait till you have seen
> The shadows dance, and there I'll be."

(*Ch'ao Tien-tzu.* 1425.2)

Disregarding the anachronism of the lighted match below, I hear echoes in "Keeping the Tryst" of Robert Browning's "Meeting at Night," second stanza:

> Then a mile of warm-scented beach;
> Three fields to cross till a farm appears;
> A tap on the pane, a quick sharp scratch
> And blue spurt of a lighted match,

---

[14] *Mao Shih,* no. 76. My translation.

夜深深靜悄。明朗朗月高。小書院無人到。書生今夜且休睡着。有句話低低道。不須輕敲。我來時將花樹兒搖。你可便記着。便休要忘了。影兒動。咱來到。半扇兒窗檻。

帶月披星擔驚怕。久立紗窗下。等候他。驀聽得門外地皮兒踏。則道是冤家。原來風動茶蘼架。

冷冷清清人寂靜。斜把鮫綃憑。和淚聽。驀聽得門外地皮兒鳴。則道是多情。卻原來翠竹把紗窗映。

And a voice less loud, through its joys and
    fears
Than the two hearts beating each to each.

The next two trysting songs by Shang T'ing belong together because the young woman is in each case waiting in vain for her lover, and because they also share not only the same dénouement but two lines almost verbatim. These two songs (like the two that follow) could well be a doublet (two attempts at writing essentially the same verse), but this is nearly impossible to determine with certainty. Songs from Xanadu were composed for the most part by little-known persons; they were immediately part of the public domain, to be copied, altered, and imitated by anyone. The scholar who would draw biographical conclusions based on the contents of songs attributed to a particular person, is, for the most part, pursuing an *ignis fatuus*. (See *Songs from Xanadu*, chapter 3, for one of the very few exceptions.)

Late, beneath the stars and moon,
Under the window, braving fear,
I stand, wait, I hope to hear
Him coming soon.
Hark! Outside the gate there comes a sound—
My lover's footsteps on the ground?
Ah, no, it's not—
The wind is rustling in the garden plot!

                    (*Pu-pu chiao*. 63.1)

Still and lonely night, chill and clear.
Brushing the curtains

Of "mermaid gauze" aside,
She swallows a sob, stifles a tear,
For suddenly she strains to hear
Her lover's footsteps on the ground—
Blue bamboos shadowing her screen outside
Are rustling; there is no other sound.

(*Pu-pu chiao.* 62.5)

If the young woman awaiting her lover in the first examples is a bit too timid and supine for the reader's taste, let me introduce a rather more froward miss in the next two, by the same poet:

Elegant slippers with "twined root" trim.
Elfin feet bound wondrously slim.
A willowy waist—
Slowly her Golden Lotus shoes are shed;
Languorously she tilts her head:
A child, before others acting shy,
She pretends to have trouble with her
    waistband tie.

(*Pu-pu Chiao.* 62.3)

Adorable slippers enclose
Tiny bound feet in their white hose—
As they make their way so quickly here.
You've deceived your parents, impudent one,
So with your lover you're most severe—
Yet see how rapidly your waistband's undone!

(*Pu-pu Chiao.* 62.4)[15]

裏解花裙兒帶。
小小鞋兒白腳帶。
纏得堪人愛。
疾快來。
瞞着爹娘做些兒怪。
你罵喫敲才。
百忙

裙兒扣。
小小鞋兒連根繡。
纏得幫兒瘦。
腰似柳。
款撒金蓮懶抬頭。
那孩兒見人羞。
推把

Many love songs from Xanadu, as is apparent
from the great similarities of theme and treatment,
belong to conventional genres and should not neces-
sarily be considered as related to the poet's own
situation or experiences. The women you have met
so far, and will continue to read about, have almost
all been generalized females—those who were given
names seem without exception to have been famous
entertainer-courtesans. This is what makes the last
young lady I will introduce so very striking: she is
not generalized; she has a name (Miss Tung)[16] and a
profession (embroiderer). She is not a langorous
cyprian, nor yet a famous beauty of the past; she is
a humble seamstress. Instead of surrounding her
with the opulent accoutrements commonly dwelt on
as a setting for women in bedchambers (gauzy cloth-
ing, scented bed-hangings, "incense seals," bronze

---

[15]We tend to think of Chinese footbinding as having
happened all at once and having been crippling from the
beginning, but the composer of this song takes pains to have
his young lady tripping along quite quickly to her tryst. It is
possible that for a long time it was simply the slimming effect
of wrapping normal feet tightly that was considered erotic by
those who fancied such things. Also, there seem to have been
several styles in small feet. I refer the student to *CYSC* 475.4,
titled "Beautiful Little Feet," where Golden Lotus shoes are
seen kicking the hems of trousers. There is what appears to
be slimming hosiery involved (I can make very little out of that
verse), but no wrappings are mentioned, and the total effect of
this footwear is of "soft-jade hooks," "tiny tusks of new moons,"
and "narrow little bow- shaped shoes" (1445.1). It is obvious that,
unlike the blunt, crushing contraptions we have all seen pictures
of from late nineteenth-century and early twentieth-century China,
these shoes were turned up in some exaggerated fashion at the
toes—a style popular in the West from time to time.

[16] Possibly Tung Mei-hsiang.

animal-forms as braziers, jade curtain-hooks, tiny slippers, cloudy hair, and silkworm brows), the composer focuses on a single object, the embroidery needle, and a single action, its use. His uniform poetic conceit throughout six of the eight songs is the girl's lovelorn condition being aggravated by the very connubial symbols and auspicious phrases that her needle embroiders—presumably preparing someone else's trousseau.

There are no other songs extant quite like these two sets of four; both are entitled "For Miss Tung the Broiderer" *(Wei Tung chen-ku tso)*. Set 1 is done to the song matrix *Wu-yeh-erh,* and set 2 to the matrix *T'ien-ching-sha.* Since the publications in which they first appeared are not available to me, I cannot guess what the original order of the songs was, nor indeed whether set 1 was the original, and set 2 emulated it, or the reverse. My first speculation (and I shall indulge in a number of them in this section) is that the composer of what is now the second set in *CYSC* was charmed by the first set's image of the needle as an almost independent agent adding to the burden of Miss Tung's lovesickness, and he composed four songs (to a different matrix), all of which include mention of the needle itself. Set 1 (whoever composed it, and there is argument even about the correct name of the probable composer) features the needle only in 1128.1 and 1128.4. Songs 2 and 3 of the set are simply lovesickness songs; in fact, I included number 3 (1128.3) above in my section devoted to that subject.

相
思
病
。
萬
種
情
。
幾
度
海
山
盟
。
誰
薄
倖
。
誰
至
誠
。
更
能
行
。
到
底
如
何
離
影
。

Before I commit myself to any more specula-tions,[17] let me remind the reader of some basic facts about Chinese poetry. Compact Chinese *shih* poetry will seldom devote precious syllabic space to un-needed pronouns; *tz'u* lyrics are somewhat more generous with them, and songs from Xanadu still more so. Nonetheless, you are seldom absolutely sure when reading Chinese verse whether (for exam-ple) there is an omniscient narrator transmitting the scene and its images to you, or whether you should think of the verse as coming from the mind—per-haps even the lips—of the protagonist or the author or both. In order to clarify things for those who don't read Chinese, and to some extent justify my specu-lations, I am going to do something I rarely indulge in—translate a poem into word-for-word English:

> Lovesick;
> Ten thousand kinds of emotion.
> How many oaths by seas and mountains?
> Who faithless?
> Who perfectly sincere?
> Can change be made?
> Truly, how to leave a shadow?

> (Lu Chih-an. *Wu-yeh-erh.* 1128.2)

I usually steer clear of such renderings: since the original reads smoothly, why should not its English

---

[17] I've already sneaked in a couple without confession: that Miss Tung was real and not just a happy inspiration on the part of the songwriter, and that said Miss Tung is plying her trade creating a trousseau for someone else.

version do likewise? Some ambiguity of voice has
both charm and compact pictorial power in the
original, but to me the literal translation above
sounds a bit like Og of the Cave People practising
a peculiarly precocious kind of English. Unlike Chi-
nese, our language is so constructed that it is always
giving the show away. Gender is revealed because
the translator has to choose between *he, she,* and *it*
(not so with the rather precious *one,* which Norman
influence I normally consider unsuited to what
were, after all, popular songs). English verbs, like it
or not, will generally reveal whether one person or
more than one is involved. Since I must believe the
composer of this song, and those who wrote all the
other songs from Xanadu, were composing singable
pieces of their language—complete with rhyme and
meter and using all the poetic resources of their
craft—to do this composer justice I must use a con-
gruent kind of English, thus:

> With love I am heartsore;
> Ten thousand emotions are confused.
> By the timeless seas and hills
> Again and again we swore.
> Was the faithless one you?
> Would another have stayed true?
> Can I put you out of mind?
> Can anyone leave his shadow behind?

Unlike Og, I have committed myself. I am inside
Miss Tung's mind—she has (had?) a lover and most
of her questions are put (in her mind) to him;
they are not simply invitations to abstract philo-
sophical discussion, for which they might possibly

be mistaken in the word-for-word version. There is ambiguity in the original, and I hope I have preserved some of it ("Would another have stayed true?" What other? Miss Tung? Another lover?).

I've given you a real, live Miss Tung, and she has a lover who appears to be less than dependable. Thinking about him distracts her from her craft:

> It can tell
> Tales to break the heart,
> Poems to wring the bowels as well.
> Jet-black thread can even ape the art
> Of drunken calligraphy.
> Despite its golden words,
> Its lyrics woven like silk brocade,
> No match for spring mating-flights of birds
> Is this needle of her trade.

(1128.1)

> The priceless golden phrase,
> The sentiments of olden days,
> In the sewing suddenly appear
> To be heart-rending sighs.
> (The deeper the love
> The more we agonize.)
> No loving friend is here—
> What inducement then
> To pick up the broidery needle again?

(1128.4)

Unlike the first poem above, these last two pieces seem to feature an omniscient observer; he knows not only what she thinks, and what she does, he

心間事。
腸斷時。
醉墨寫烏絲。
千金字。
織錦詞。
繡針兒。
不比鴛兒燕子。

千金字。
萬古心。
翻作斷腸吟。
恩情厚。
怨恨深。
不知音。
誰會重拈繡針。

knows what she can be stirred by and even offers generalities that we may better see how well he understands the situation ("The deeper the love / The more we agonize"). Who then is this percipient fellow? Well, if you were not disturbed by my bringing Miss Tung to life, I trust you're also generous enough not to deny her a flesh-and-blood lover—the one who does in fact write these songs "For Miss Tung the Broiderer." Is it the shadowy composer Lu Chih-an (Lu Chih-hsüan?)? The editors of *CYSC* acknowledge that they know nothing about him, but they believe the two different given names actually belong to the same person (see *CYSC*, p. 1122). I will avoid that question entirely and fall back on a few acceptable conjectures to see if we can evoke (even if we cannot name) a suitable lover for our seamstress.

The households of well-to-do Chinese families in the past were equipped with numerous servants—from the boy who slept by the gate to admit late revelers to domestics and ladies' maids who saw to wardrobe and other needs of *Lao t'ai-t'ai* (the matriarch of the house), her daughters, and a multitude of female relatives. One need only have read *Chin-p'ing Mei (Golden Lotus)* or *Hung-lou Meng (Dream of the Red Chamber)* to realize that such serving-maids were fair game (sexually speaking) for young scions of the family. I imagine the situation in this respect was much like that in the aristocratic English manor houses of past centuries. There were doubtless customary rules about which liaisons were allowable and which were not; their issue were probably considered a charge upon the clan and given some sort of support in the large menial demi-monde that orbited any great family. However, marriage—or indeed any quasi-legal arrangement—was certainly considered impossible; the social gap was just too wide to allow of such a bridge. But social custom and legal barriers are notoriously impotent to prevent people "falling in love."

As you have already guessed, I have chosen an offspring of the family that employs Miss Tung as broiderer to be both the composer of the first four songs and Miss Tung's "loving friend." I know many literary critics would shoot my "intentional fallacy" to bits: not only have I speculated on the author's intention in writing these songs, I have created a composer, his mistress, and an entire extended Chinese family! *Mea maxima culpa!*

But my confession of guilt is perfunctory—as so many such confessions are. Until I stumbled on Miss Tung I had never read songs with such an unusual overall tone, nor are there any others in the entire *CYSC* dedicated by name to a menial. The vocabulary of the first set of four songs is relatively artless, the composer's conceit so naturally matched with his subject that I was believing in both Miss Tung and her lover before I could stop myself.

The second set of four is another case: In these I find the composer too taken with his own cleverness to qualify as Miss Tung's tender lover. The writer of the first set, it seems to me, is very aware that the affair can never lead to a formal arrangement— much as both of them might want it—and this lends an extra piquancy to his songs. The first set's concern is with the emotions of Miss Tung, neatly expressed through the agency of her embroidery needle in two of the compositions. The second composer appears overly anxious to work the needle image into all four of his songs; Miss Tung's emotions are secondary for him:

Deep in the night and alone, I see
Her trimming a pair of shoes.
Not a word has she said to me,
And yet I know
She's longing for affection—
This, despite her outward show
Of fierce rejection.
The *girl* pretends petulance; just the same,
Her *needle* is sewing the rascal's name!

(1128.5)

With her needle she can rouge
The blossom's subtle hue: she creates
The thin green natural broidery—
Criss-cross fronds of the weeping willow tree.
But swallows and orioles together with their
    mates
Touch her heartfelt loneliness,
And then her busy needle pauses, motionless.

(1129.1)

Jade-white like spring shoots,
Her fingers cramped by their occupation.
Her brows—distant mountain ranges
Drawn down in concentration.
A thousand fruitless worries
Have made her cross—
Then, far off, someone has sung
A verse of "Mai-hua-sheng,"

夜深時獨繡羅鞋。不言語倒在人懷。做意兒將人不採。甚娘作怪。繡針兒簽着敲才。

海棠輕染胭脂。綠楊亂撒青絲。對對鴛兒燕子。傷心獨自。繡針兒停待多時。

And even the eye of her needle
Rejects the floss!

(1129.2)

Cold, all alone, she keeps
To the chamber where she sleeps.
Depressed, she'll sometimes lean
Beside her gauzy window-screen.
Then, staring sightlessly, she rests upon her
    bed—
For a moment, as her spirit seems to hang
Outside herself—her needle writes
    "Mei-hsiang."

(1129.3)

So common was the name Mei-hsiang ("Plum-fragrance") for a maidservant that virtually every female servant in any Yuan drama will be so called. The implication here seems to be that Miss Tung has mindlessly stitched the characters for her own name (presumably the name of the seamstress has no place on the work she does for the family that employs her), thus emphasizing her menial status and perhaps indicating her unconscious wish that she were the one for whom this embroidery was destined.

While the first set of songs is noteworthy for its restrained vocabulary, untranslated elements in 1129.3 above have Miss Tung keeping to her "orchid" chamber and resting upon the "embroidered" couch—epithets suitable for the courtesan but hardly for a sewing maid.

Of course, all my speculation to the contrary, the same man could have written both sets: over a

玉纖屈損春蔥。遠山壓損眉峰。早是閒愁萬種。忽聽得賣花聲送。繡針兒不待穿絨。

冷清清獨守蘭房。悶懨懨倚定紗窗。呆答孩搭伏定繡床。一會家神魂飄蕩。繡針兒簽這梅香。

period of time the composer may have become more and more the verse-monger and less and less the lover—after all, we understand as little about the process of falling out of love as we do about falling in love.

To have found embedded in Yuan dynasty song-poetry all the nuances of the most human and most powerful of mankind's emotions (including the maladroit amours and ribald mishaps treated in the next chapter) just as they appear in Western literature is a source of great satisfaction to me. I am hard put to say exactly why this should be so, but in part it is because my faith that human beings are much more alike than they are different is confirmed by these observations, and I have a gut feeling that such basic similarities stand in constant need of iteration.

2

Songs of Mockery and Parody

The world is a perpetual caricature of itself.

G. Santayana

Maladroit amours and ribald mishaps have played a large part in Western prose and poetry from Greek comedic drama through Boccaccio to the present. The preceding chapter introduced a similar vein in Yuan dynasty songs, with Wang Ho-ch'ing's airy depreciation of the legend of Su Ch'ing and Shuang Chien, his society's most famous romantic love story. The irrepressible Wang (who wrote the song about the love note handicapped by bad handwriting) also composed a very much broader piece featuring the ludicrous situation in which a lover's flight of passion is brought heavily (pun intended) back to earth. The following song is a satire of numberless Yuan

夜深交頸効鴛鴦。錦被翻紅浪。雨歇雲收那情況。難當。一翻翻在人身上。偌長

偌大。偌粗偌胖。壓匾沈東陽。

招招拈拈寒賤。偷偷抹抹姻緣。幕天席地枕頭兒磚。或是廚灶底。馬欄邊。忍些

兒卻。怕敢氣喘。

songs in which every lover is a handsome young man and every mistress a willow-waisted beauty. Its very title sets the tone for this entire chapter—"Fat Courtesan":

> Throughout the night we love-ducks played.
> The ripples on our pond were made
> By a heaving crimson counterpane.
> But having done with clouds and rain,
> I find it hard to bear
> When, still asleep, she rolls upon me there—
> So tall, so big, so thick, so fat—
> Like Shen Tung-yang I'm pressed quite flat!

(*Hsiao-t'ao hung.* 44.1)

Wang Ho-ch'ing was not, however, the only composer to see the farcical side of sexual activity quite divorced from falling in love. Throughout the large group of anonymous compositions in *CYSC* are scattered a number of mildly ribald songs which do not even pretend to be talking about romantic love—only sexual adversities and the accidents attending stealthy amours. They range from the slightly comic to rather broad slapstick. The following are good examples:

> Pinched by wretched poverty,
> My couplings suffer uncertainty.
> Usually, heaven's our chamber, earth's our bed,
> With only a brick beneath the head.

But, once behind the cookhouse stove,
And once in the horse's pen—
Though we had to be careful of our panting
    then!

(Anon. *Hung Hsiu-hsieh.* 1692.2)

I choose a text,
Trim the silver lamp for light and feign
To read. The woman, then, with arms like iron
    chain,
Pins me to my chair.
I suggest she might
Brew us both a pot of tea,
Or, failing that, sew something she could wear.
She replies instead:
"First things first, let's go to bed."

(Anon. *Hung Hsiu-hsieh.* 1692.4)

    Two pages of these songs (five of which are translated below) form an interesting group sharing repeated use of entire lines and phrases in differing settings. They are, I suspect, the results of a rowdy party at which everyone was required to use the same tune *(Hung Hsiu-hsieh* "Red Slippers"), and different rhymes, to sing of misadventures related to sexual activity. Songfests of this sort were common in affluent Yuan society, and occasionally some of their creations are preserved in *CYSC* among the works of various writers (see chapter 3), but seldom is a whole set—apparently each piece being done

不甫能尋得箇題目。點銀燈推看文書。被肉鐵索夫人緊繘住。又使得他煎茶去。

又使得他做衣服。倒熬得我先睡去。

by a different composer—found together in this
fashion:

I'd never set my hand
To secret love affairs before.
But now the scuffing sound of slippers
Almost at the door!
Leave by the entry, you'll be seen—
Try the window, they will hear . . .
Now all my new bravado's turned to fear!

(1692.3)

背地裏些兒歡笑。手梢兒何曾湯著。只聽得擦擦鞋鳴早來到。又那裏挨窗兒聽。

倚門兒瞧。把我一箇敢心都諕了。

I opened up the red couch-drapery
And stooped to touch the inlaid bed.
Hoping so to "light the silver lamp with thee,"
I moved my feet with such a careful tread
The slipper soles scarce touched the floor.
But then spoke that accusing tongue
Of the squeaking swinging door!

(1692.6)

手約開紅羅帳。款抬身擦下牙床。低歡會共你著銀釭。輕輕的鞋底兒放。腳不敢

把地皮兒湯。又早被這告舌頭門扇兒響。

Parting the curtains cautiously,
Lightly and most carefully
Groping for her inlaid bed,
Suddenly, on a chestnut-burr
My bare foot did tread!
My wits were scattered,
My courage shattered,
While from all this came
Noise to put a thunderclap to shame!

(1693.1)

款款的分開羅帳。輕輕的擦下牙床。栗子皮踏著不隄防。驚得膽喪。諕得魂揚。

I woke around third watch or so
To grope about my bed
And brushed against something—What do
   you know?
His drunken wife was under the spread!
Oh, this is bad, we'd both regret . . .
But how to avoid the catastrophe?
By this time I was so upset
That I fumbled for the chamber-pot
Pretending I had to pee!

(1692.5)

You've been absent quite a bit.
Now you've returned but not your wit.
So a drunken lady's in your bed
Don't lie sidewise (?), don't pretend you're
   dead.
Go back to sleep for as long as it takes.
She's bound to leave you as soon as she wakes!

(1693.2)

Notice that the last song does not construct a new scene but directs itself to the contents of the previous one and the supposed plight of its composer—a rare event in Yuan songs. The whole set generates a sense of immediacy and fundamental (if deficient) humanity seldom to be found in Chinese verse.

I have spoken to colleagues much more widely read in T'ang *shih* poetry and Sung *tz'u* poetry than I, and they tell me that though satirical pieces are not unknown to either genre, Mongol dynasty songs appear to contain more, and more elaborate,

便是震天雷不恁響。

恰睡到三更前後。款款的擦下床頭。不隄防殢酒夫人被窩兒裏搜。這場事無乾淨。

這場事怎干休。諕得我摸盆兒推淨手。

雖是間阻了。咱十朝五夜。你根前沒半米兒心別。不甫能帶酒的夫人睡著些。休死勢。莫伴斜。直睡到他覺來時回去也。

十指如枯筍。和袖捧金樽。搊殺銀箏字不眞。揉癢天生鈍。縱有相思淚痕。索把拳頭揾。

lampooning than any other verse-form that precedes or succeeds them. A bantering tone seems to be integral to the song form itself, which we know was extremely hospitable to non-traditional subject matter and ironic treatment of it. None of the songs above is designated a satire by its title (indeed, only Wang's "Fat Courtesan" has any title at all). However, there is an entire class of songs with titles including the words "satire" (ch'ao), "ridicule" (chi), "play upon" so-and-so (hsi), or sometimes "sigh over" something or another (t'an), which latter often turns out to be just as satirical as the first three classes. Only in songs from Xanadu do we have dozens of specimens of this kind of Chinese humor: examples range from the pawky to the scholarly and subtle; their quality ranges from the clever to the cruel.

Since the reader has already experienced the disparaging tone of some songs about courtesans, let me begin discussion of satirical pieces with this gentle one on a member of the oldest profession who has a bad habit. It is titled (once again, presumably by the composer himself) "Bald Fingertips" (though in one collection it is known as "Twitting a Singing-Girl for Her Bitten Fingernails"). It is obviously, therefore, a "satire," by perhaps the best known ch'ü composer of them all, Kuan Han-ch'ing:

Each finger is a tipless bamboo shoot.
To offer drinks she hides them in her sleeve.
Pluck as they may, they cannot play a lute.
So blunt, poor things, no itch can they relieve.

Alas, if tears are shed for lovers missed,
They're brushed away by a small clenched fist.

(*Tsui Fu-kuei.* 155.5)

In addition to this mild and apparently sympa-
thetic banter over bitten fingernails, there are
numerous other songs from Xanadu deriding nearly
anything you care to name: "Twitting One Whose
Beloved Courtesan Was Stolen by Another," "Lam-
poon of Youth," "Satirical Argument over Which
Client Is Best Loved by a Singing-girl," "Satire on
Courtesans Playing Football," "Ridicule of One
Ch'u-yi" (courtesan friend of Ch'ao Chi), "Maid
Tells the Master His Wife Is Drunk in the Women's
Quarters," "Return of an Emperor to His Home
Village as Seen Through the Eyes of a Village
Bumpkin," "On a Sick-Drunk Courtesan," "On a
Sleepy Courtesan," "On the Worst Performing
Troupe in the Land" (including a male lead who "has
a body as gross as a water-buffalo and a voice
hoarse as the howls of a homeless dog"). I'm mildly
surprised to note that there is, to my knowledge,
only one satirical song in *CYSC* about monks (1235.1)
and none about doctors—both these callings are
regularly burlesqued in the musical drama that was
contemporaneous with the songs from Xanadu.
However, other characters that have been the butt of
much humor in the West are also to be found as
targets in Xanadu: There is the liar, the fop, the
womanizer, the pompous official—all standard ob-
jects of ridicule—and here is one on the miser:

Ridiculing the Skinflint

He'd take clay from a swallow's beak,
Shave iron from a pin, or peel
Gilt, no matter how thin,
From a Buddha statue's cheek—
Even from nothing he'd find something to
    steal!
He would get
A pea from the crop of a quail,
Carve a steak from the leg of an egret—
Even the oil in the gut of a fly
Isn't safe from this old guy!

(Anon. *Tsui t'ai-p'ing.* 1664.3)

Below is another which also relies on elabora-
tion of eccentric behavior for its humor:

Twitting the Teller of Tall Tales

In Easton a certain citizen
Had a Phoenix born to his hen!
In Southville there was a paradox,
Someone's horse turned into an ox!
August is the month to wear fur coats,
On a pile of tile you can plant a tree,
A dry gulch[1] is good for sailing boats.
Our dumplings are bigger than soup tureens;
We grow barrel-sized aubergines.

(Anon. *Wu Yeh-erh.* 1726.4)

There is a long song *(lien-t'ao)* by Ma Chih-yüan
poking fun at a horse-fancier who has lent his favorite

奪泥燕口。削鐵鍼頭。刮金佛面細搜求。無中覓有。鵪鶉嗉裏尋豌豆。鷺鷥腿上

劈精肉。蚊子腹內刳脂油。虧老先生下手。

東村裏雞生鳳。南莊上馬變牛。六月裏裏皮裘。瓦壟上宜栽樹。陽溝裏好駕舟。

甕來大肉饅頭。俺家的茄子大如斗。

mount to a friend and is having agonized second thoughts about what will happen to the beloved beast at the hands of the borrower.[2] Another, written by Chung Ssu-ch'eng, is a rueful satire on ugliness of visage—particularly his own homeliness. He includes tongue-in-cheek examples of the ill-favored throughout Chinese history who succeeded despite their lack of beauty. It was Chung Ssu-ch'eng, by the way, who chose *Ch'ou-chai* or "Homeliness House" for the name of his studio. Not all of these pieces include the words "ridicules," "satires," or "laughs at" in their titles, but as we've noted, the titles of so many songs from Xanadu are mere afterthoughts, often given them by later song collectors. The contents of songs about all the topics above, however, are unmistakably satirical and burlesque. As the reader can see, the courtesan sorority comes in for a great share of ridicule, but then, few professions are completely spared, including that of teaching. The teacher in one satire is made to complain that his students lack diligence, but the students retort that the pedagogue can't stop droning on. Even the trades take barbs: there is a long song titled "The Mendacious Cobbler" and another, translated below, called something like "Banter about a Man with Worn-out Shoes." Why footwear and its makers should be accorded so much satirical attention in song is obscure to me, but the farcical tone is perfectly clear.

---

[1] *Yang-kou:* "open ditch." There may be some play on words here; Yang-kou was the name of a famous fighting cock.

[2] See *Songs*, pp. 27–30, for a translation.

兩腮綻開。底破幫兒壞。幾番修補費錢財。還不徹王皮債。不敢大步闊行。只得徐行短邁。怕的是狼牙石龜背階。上臺基左。歪右歪。又不敢着棺排。只好倒吊起朝陽曬。

Both vamps'
Stitches burst,
Their soles are bad but the thongs are the
    worst.
So many patches at such great cost
All sign of the original leather is lost.
They dare not freely walk or stride,
But in wincing, mincing footsteps slide.
Their wearer's greatest menace will
Be the wolf-toothed stone
Or the turtle-backed sill.
And when he stands on the slightest height
He tilts to the left or sags to the right.
He dare not put them on a last to dry
But carefully hangs them with their soles to
    the sky.

(Anon. *Ch'ao Tien-tzu.* 1687.3)

A curious topic for the exercise of wit, perhaps, but when your burlesque tradition includes "On a Tall Girl," "Ridiculing a Man Sleeping on the Table," "Man with Only Three Fingers on His Right Hand," and "The Wry-Mouthed Singing-Girl," (this last contains such deathless lines as "She can stare straight ahead yet spit to the left"!), what topic could seem strange?

The substantial group of songs that are truly parodic should be included in this chapter as well. Parodies imply that the listener-reader is already very familiar with the particular literary form, tone, or cliché the parody burlesques, and enjoyment of the piece is determined by one's ability to contrast the obliquity of the parody with the right angles of the original.[3] For example, one of the favorite images in both Chinese poetry and painting (see chapter 3) is that of the sturdy, independent fisherman plying his trade. In graphic art, two or three thin black lines indicate his boat, mast, and cane fishing pole; a dab with the frayed tip of a brush, and there, hunched against the snow, appears the fisherman in his rush cloak. His presence immediately makes optical sense of the rest of an almost completely white sheet of paper. Similarly, in the art of poetry, it was enough to mention him—alone, earning his livelihood in the middle of a snowy river—to make emotional sense of a self-sufficient life, free of the taxes and restrictions which the poet and his readers knew only too well. There is a well-known short song that parodies this poetic cliché by putting the composer inside the mind of the fisher. There, the audience discovers the fisher completely lacking interest in the picture he makes—all *he* is thinking of is home fires and warm hangings on the walls.

In the long song that follows below, the element of parody lies in the fact that the corpus of Chinese poetry is simply stuffed with allusions to the good omens of snow. In a society founded on intensive agriculture, a heavy snow-pack on distant mountains means a well-watered bumper crop in the valley the following summer. The composer of "In Dispraise of Snow," however, will trade all the good omens for one good night's sleep, and pretends that Meng Hao-jan, and other poets who praised snow,

---

[3] See Wang Ho-ch'ing's "Fat Couple" in chapter 1.

不呈六出祥。豈應三白瑞。易添身上冷。能使腹中肌。有甚稀奇。無主向沿街墜。不着人到處飛。暗敲窗有影。無形。偷入戶。潛縱躡跡。才上茅庵草舍。又鑽入破壁疏籬。似楊花滾滾輕狂勢。你幾曾見貴公子錦裯繡褥。你多曾伴老漁翁箬笠蓑衣。爲飄風胡作胡爲。怕騰雲相趁相隨。只着你凍的箇孟浩然掙掙癡癡。只着

were not so much inspired as put upon by the white stuff:

Yi-chih Hua

You're not the good "six-point augury"
Nor propitious "Three-White Jade" of
      prophecy;[4]
You're much too quick to help the body lose
      its heat,
And often press us hard to find enough to eat—
Virtues neither fine nor rare.
Masterless, your snowflakes fill our lanes,
Without our leave they flutter everywhere—
Formless shadows tapping on our window
      panes.
They penetrate the household gate
And hide all signs that men went there.

Liang-chou

Blanketing alike grass huts and Buddhist
      halls,
You probe the gap-toothed fence and ruined
      walls—
Every puff
Is like the weightless madness of whirling
      willow-fluff.
You seldom visit brocade coats,
But gather on rush-capes in fishers' boats.
Now stirring, now resting—whither the wind
      blows,

---

[4] Doubtless referring to a peasant omen like "Let the land be three times white / That will see the wheat crop right."

你逼的箇林和靖，欽欽歷歷。只着你阻的箇韓退之，哭哭啼啼。更長。漏遲。被窩中無半點兒因他和氣。惱人眠。攪人睡。似你那冷燥皮膚似鐵石。着我怎敢相偎。冬酒債因他累。千里關山被你迷。似這等浪蕊閑花也不是久長計。儘飄零數日。掃除做一堆。我將你溫不熱薄情化做了水。

Or leaping or trailing when a dark cloud snows.
Was it not you who froze
Poor Meng Hao-jan, that infatuated man?
And oppressed
Poor Lin Ho-ch'ing, respectful of you in every-
    thing?
And hampered the weeping Han T'ui-chih?[5]
And does not snow
Make night-watches long,
And the water-clocks drip slow?
Snow drains all trace of heat from comforter
    and sheet.
Snow can rouse those who soundly sleep—
It also vexes those who only drowse.
Snow, your cold, dry skin is comfortless,
And with its feel of stone or steel
Does not invite my warm caress.

Wei
All winter long my wine-debts rose;
Roads and passes were obscured by snows.
What's more—
Your waves of feckless blossoms are short on
    constancy,
So all the flakes of some days past
Will be swept into a pile by me;
I need only make them slightly warm
And your fickle substance will change its
    form!

(T'ang Yi-fu. *Yi-chih Hua lien-t'ao*. 1185.1)

---

[5] Each of these famous poets had written verses about snow.

* * *

I am not sure how one should classify the following
pieces; they are not parodies of any recognizable
type, but their obvious tongue-in-cheek wittiness,
addressed to both metaphysics and mythical mon-
sters, reminds one forcibly of the "ridicules" and
"satires" described at the beginning of this chapter.
The comparison of traditional Chinese cosmology
with an inflated ball shares the eccentric humor
found in many burlesque songs from Xanadu:

Inflated Ball

When the primal force of all
Finished wrapping chaos 'round,
It rejoiced in rotund girth.
So does this air-filled leather ball.
Now, when such an object's found
Lying on the sporting ground,
Like the heart's tumescent woes
It's better kicked away through purple clouds
Than rolled about on dusty earth!

(Chang K'o-chiu. *Ch'en-tsui Tung-feng*. 932.2)

The leviathan was used in early Chinese phi-
losophy to stand for dimensions which human be-
ings could not encompass with their limited minds;
Chiang T'ai-kung was the sage who sat fishing by
the Fan river until such time as the great King Wen
should come to seek his advice:

元氣初包混沌。皮囊自喜團圝。閒田地著此身。絕世慮縈方寸。圓滿也不必煩人。

一腳騰空上紫雲。強似向紅塵亂滾。

鋪眉苫眼早三公。裸袖揎拳享萬鍾。胡言亂語成時用。大綱來都是烘。

公怎釣。夯風濤。脊梁上輕負着蓬萊島。萬里夕陽錦背高。翻身猶恨東洋小。太

勝神鰲。

The Leviathan

The Monster Turtle's not so great as he
Who causes tidal waves upon the sea:
From whose colossal carcass rise
The storied Isles of Paradise.
The far-off evening sun sets in
His great brocaded dorsal fin.
His mighty bulk resents that he's
Restricted by the Eastern Seas.
Chiang T'ai-kung, who caught a king,
Could never land this monstrous thing!

(Wang Ho-ching. *Po Pu-tuan.* 45.2)

* * *

Finally, it would seem to stand to reason that sooner or later the tenor of the times in which they lived should become subject matter for a generation of composers who grew up used to a tradition of satirical song. But the curious fact is that among the thousands of extant songs from Xanadu (roughly 5,500 of them—long and short—in *CYSC*) I have found only three which seem clearly to satirize the age. Let me give you here the first stanza of one, the title of which leaves no doubt of its subject. Attributed to Chang Ming-shan, it is called *Chi-shih*, or "Lampooning the Times"—though I prefer to translate its title in the words of Cicero:

O Tempora! O Mores!

The hooded eye, the beetling brow
Hold our highest offices now.

Bared bicep and naked fist
Are what make men the wealthiest.
Our present age does so esteem
Unbridled speech and baseless theme—
We're nothing but a noisy flock![6]

(*Shui Hsien-tzu.* 1282.3)

The other two satires-on-the-times are anony-
mous and appear to be doublets, so alike are they in
their wording and sequence of ideas. (In a collection
like *CYSC,* constituted of no less than one hundred
seventeen different song collections, doublets and
indeed triplets and quadruplets are not uncommon.)

Feelings about Ambition

Be unread to get ahead.
Be illiterate and benefit!
Nowadays, to gain men's praise
Simply be inadequate.
Heaven won't discriminate
Between the wicked and the great,
Nor have we ever had
Rules to tell good men from bad.
Men cheat the good,
They scorn the poor,
And the learned trip
On their scholarship.

---

[6] The second stanza consists mainly of allusions to great men and
events of the past. It does not take well to translation.

不讀書最高。不識字最好。不曉事倒有人誇俏。老天不肯辨清濁。好和歹沒條道。

善的人欺。貧的人笑。讀書人都累倒。立身則小學。修身則大學。智和能都不及。

鴨青鈔。

不讀書有權。不識字有錢。不曉事倒有人誇薦。老天只恁忒心偏。賢和愚無分辨。折挫英雄。消磨良善。越聰明越運蹇。志高如魯連。德過如閔騫。依本分只落的人輕。

So practise no calligraphy,
Great Learning[7] or epigraphy!
Intelligence and competence
Now count for less than copper pence.

(Anon. *Ch'ao Tien-tzu.* 1688.2)

Thoughts on Ambition

The unread will get ahead,
The illiterate will benefit,
Incompetence leads to prominence!
Old Heaven is so obstinate
He'll not distinguish mean from great;
He brings about catastrophe
To knave and hero equally,
And the brighter men are, the worse their fate!
Lu Chung-lien and Min-tzu Ch'ien[8]—
Aspiring and moral men,
To noble obligations sworn—
Are nowadays held up to scorn.

(Anon. *Ch'ao T'ien-tzu.* 1688.1)

All of us hope to discover in works of literature something significant about the age in which they were produced, but most of us in our soberer moments realize that the writer, being an artist, is almost

---

[7] The *Ta-hsüeh (Great Learning)* was a pre-Han collection of Confucian homilies.

[8] Pre-Ch'in models for lofty ambition. The former was perhaps the only figure in the *Chan-kuo Ts'e* that the Confucians approved of; the latter was a disciple of Confucius.

by definition one who views his age with a kind of idiosyncratic vision. That fact, indeed, is what gives artists unique value. They will always tell us *something* about their era, but only in the most tangential fashion, and if their works be wrenched to prove sociological or political theories or "facts," a great deal of possibly pernicious nonsense will be written.

The three songs above have several times been cited by Chinese scholars as literary proof of general governmental depravity in the age of the Mongols. I find their arguments quite unconvincing. Would they also insist, I wonder, that the presence of two satirical songs on shoes and shoemakers (see 1687.3 above) implied that the cobblers' guild was corrupt and their products shoddy? I certainly would not contend that serious poetic indictments of the Mongols might not appear in *CYSC*—quite the contrary. There could have been many literate Jurcheds of the thoroughly sinicized Chin dynasty (the group most directly affected by the Mongol invasion) who voiced their discontent in song. I happen to believe, however, that such compositions would be much more allusive than the three we have been considering. Though there is no way to prove it, I have a strong impression that the following is just such a song. It should be noted that the character used for the composer's surname, Ho, would be a rare one for a Han Chinese, and his other appellation, Hsi-ts'un (Westville) is quite possibly a pseudonym:

Sentinel Tower and Sunset Clouds

City wall, sentinel tower
Against a red-wrack sunset sky;
Only darkling hills supply

戍樓殘照斷霞紅。只有青山送。梨葉新來帶霜重。望歸鴻。歸鴻也被西風弄。閑愁萬種。舊遊雲夢。回首月明中。

Me their companionship.
The new pear leaves are thick with frost.[9]
I watch you, wild goose—
Wild goose on your migrant trip,
Like me, by westwinds tossed—
And a nameless anguish holds me in its grip.
Ah, once we wandered Yün-meng Park;
I turn as if to glimpse it
By moonlight, in the dark.

(Ho Hsi-ts'un. *Hsiao-t'ao Hung.* 54.1)[10]

A wild goose tossed by the winds of adversity
is to be found in many songs alluding to human
troubles of a political kind. Allusion to Yün-meng
Park summons up the ghost of Nan-T'ang Hou-chu,
a romantic figure who lost his dynasty to cruder and
more powerful forces. There are a number of such
allusive songs in *CYSC* that I have no trouble relating
to men who were part of or dependent upon the
Chin, the tribe/dynasty displaced by the Mongols.
One of the better known among such songs (357.1)
is attributed to a Uigur, Kuan Yün-shih. Titled
"Written for Another," it includes the lines: "Bat-
tling the westwind, tiny dots; / Geese returning,
waken ancient griefs of a southern kingdom."

---

[9] As J. P. Seaton pointed out to me, *fen-li* ("frosty pears") is certainly a pun for "separation."

[10] That this song is grouped with seven others, and that they are in some collections referred to as "eight scenes along the river," should not be given too much weight. Such groupings, as often as not, are made by editors for their own purposes.

I believe these and other songs like them may be true remnants of resentment against the Mongol conquerors. The authors of both of these appear to have lived early in the Yuan dynasty, when anguish over the invasions was still fresh. The most serious objection to my speculations is the fact that we have preserved in *CYSC* songs written by three Jurcheds who were mature when the Mongols invaded and who suffered in varying degrees from the event: Yuan Hao-wen, Yang Kuo, and Liu Chien-chung lost relatives or positions, yet there is not a single song by any of them that even hints at complaint against invaders from the steppes. This despite the fact that Yuan Hao-wen in his *shih* poetry (a non-song verse form) wrote a number of so-called *sang-luan* or "death and destruction" poems condemning the brutality of the Mongols and grieving over the fate of China. The fact must be faced that for much of its brief period of popularity Yuan dynasty song-poetry was by nature and by practice devoted to lighter sentiments.[11]

---

[11] There are exceptions to this, of course. See the funeral ode in chapter 1 and the songs of Chang Yang-hao in *Songs*, chapter 3.

3

Songs of Wisdom, Contemplation, and Friendship

> *How to the singer comes the song?*
> *How to the summer fields*
> *Come flowers? How yields*
> *Darkness to the happy morn?*

Richard Watson Gilder

Having pointed out in the first half of this book those topics to which songs from Xanadu pay more attention than other forms of Chinese verse, it seems proper to devote this chapter to themes that have been perennially popular throughout the history of Chinese poetry and song and remained so in the *ch'ü* genre of the Mongol era.

搬興廢東生玉兔。識榮枯西墜金烏。富貴榮華待何如。斬白蛇高祖勝。舉鼎霸王輸。都做了北邙山下土。

Memento Mori

The glories of our blood and State
Are shadows, not substantial things.
There is no armour against fate;
Death lays his icy hands on kings.

James Shirley

The Chinese were as aware as any people on earth of the irony that death's pale flag flies alike over mighty sepulchres and over dust in the potter's field; yet they behaved (as we do) as if wealth were desirable and progeny conferred a measure of immortality, even though their songs often suggested they feared otherwise:

Fortune may change from good to ill;
In the east the Moon-hare rises still.
Fame or dishonor lost or won,
Westward still sinks the Bird-of-the-sun.
What then are wealth and glory worth?
The victor once was Han Kao-tsu
Who clove the great white snake in two;
Hsiang Yü, the loser, Hegemon king
Whose strength could lift great brazen *ting*.[1]
What is left of either man
Lies buried now on Pei-mang Shan[2]—
Both bodies turned to earth!

(Anon. *Hung Hsiu-hsieh.* 1694.4)

---

[1] Large ceremonial tripods cast for dynastic prestige.

To one of them fair fortune came;
One, scarce a bushel to his name.
Does Heaven reckon wealth and fame?
At thirty-two one spent his days
Obscure, and lived in rustic ways.
By twenty-four the first had known
Rank in chancellery to the throne.
But all that's left of either man
Are buried bones on Pei-mang Shan.

(Anon. *Hung Hsiu-hsieh.* 1695.1)

一箇千鍾美祿。一箇石栗之儲。天理如何有榮枯。三十二居陋巷。二十四位中書。都做了北邙山下骨。

And there are echoes of the Preacher's views on "vanity" (*Ecclesiastes* 1,3): "What profit hath a man of all his labor which he taketh under the sun? One generation passeth away, and another generation cometh: but the earth abideth forever":

Vast the world and its forge of time:
Within that mighty firepan
Lie cooling ashes of the works of man—
So has it been since time began.
Behold, abandoned battlements
Reclaimed by mist and creeping plants,
And these: great ruins crowned by ancient
    trees.

茫茫大塊洪鑪裏。何物不寒灰。古今多少。荒煙廢壘。老樹遺臺。太行如礪。黃河如帶。等是塵埃。不須更嘆。花開花落。春去春來。

---

[2] On a hill north of the Han dynasty capital city of Loyang, the mausoleum of Prince Kung was erected in A.D. 36. For no known reason, this area, called Pei-mang Shan, then became the favored necropolis for the mighty; allusion to it testifies that death is the great leveler.

布衣中。問英雄。王圖霸業成何用。禾黍高低六代宮。楸梧遠近千官塚。一場惡夢。

"Til T'ai-shan becomes a whetstone,
The Yellow a narrow band."[3]
All things will turn to sand.
But why should I sigh?
Flowers bloom, flowers die.
Though this spring is past,
Next spring will come as did the last.

(Liu Yin. *Jen Yueh Yuan.* 72.2)

Dressed in my robes of common cloth
I question history's heroic men:
"What boots it then,
The Kingly Plan, the Tyrant's Scheme?"
High or low,
Tombs where mighty lords have lain
Now support the peasant's grain.
Far or near,
On once-grand courts' debris
The farmer tends his catalpa tree.
All history is a nightmare dream!

(Ma Chih-yüan. *Po Pu-tuan.* 253.4)

And, of course, the Chinese have never been without the hedonist reaction to life's brevity and uncertainty:

---

[3] T'ai-shan is one of the sacred mountains of China. Legend has it that a Han dynasty oath ran: "May the Han last till T'ai-shan is the size of a whetstone and the Yellow River as wide as a sash."

A Sigh Over Life

Heaps of jade,
Mounds of gold—
Then there comes a single day
And Old Death sweeps them all away!
What good are they?
Let not slip by unsung
The cloudless hour,
The day benign.
Salute the crystal cup, the amber wine,
The swaying waists,
The flashing teeth and eyes—
Ah, there's where pleasure truly lies.

(Ma Chih-yüan. *Ssu-k'uai Yü.* 238.2)

Retreat to Tranquillity

Songs dealing with this topic fall generally into two classes: self-congratulation that the persona has avoided the strains of a public career throughout his life, or relief that finally his duty is done, and he can retire from the hurly-burly. In either case the theme furnishes an excellent opportunity for self-justification by disappointed office-seekers, for those "whose minds were as full of wealth and position as their mouths were of [retiring to] mountain fastnesses and forest solitudes," to quote Cheng Ch'ien.

East beyond the Yangtse
Then west far past Ch'ang-an.
With fame the goad
My journey's gone
All around Horizon's Road—

心待足時名便足。高處苦。低處苦。

大江東去。長安西去。為功名走遍天涯路。厭舟車。喜琴書。早星星鬢影瓜田暮。

齒歌。倒大來閑快活。

白玉堆。黃金垜。一日無常果如何。良辰媚景休空過。琉璃鍾琥珀濃。細腰舞皓

綠陰茅屋兩三間。院後溪流門外山。山桃野杏開無限。怕春光虛過眼。得浮生半

日清閑。邀鄰翁爲伴。使家僮過盞。直喫的老瓦盆乾。

Resenting each carriage and boat I took,
Longing for my lute and book.
And now an evening star appears
In the blackness of my temple hair—
Sign of Shao P'ing's twilight years.[4]
But the heart completely satisfied
Knows all it needs of name and pride.
To the mighty
Come mighty blows;
And lesser folk
Suffer lesser woes.

(Hsüeh Ang-fu. *Shan-p'o Yang.* 709.3)

My Rural Home

Thatched huts in green shade—
Two or three in all.
Beyond the compound wall
A brook runs in its glade,
While outside my gate the mountains loom
And a myriad wild apricot and hill-peach
        bloom.
I fear but one thing:
Some subtle light of spring
Might elude my eye.
So I shall float with life as it goes by!
I vow to idle half of every day—
I'll seek out that old codger 'cross the way,

---

[4] Literally, "melon-field evenings." Shao P'ing (Tung-ling Hou) of the Ch'in spent his later years out of power, yet content growing his melons. He has become an eponym for withdrawal and contentment as age approaches.

Send the boy with the wine-jug by
And we'll drink our stoneware noggins dry!

(Kuan Yün-shih. _Shui Hsien-tzu._ 372.4)

State honor rolls will back my name
As do biographies for men of fame.
I _have_ from time to time
Found sagehood in a cup of wine;
Now and then,
Some verse of mine
Has contained one brilliant line
Enlightening as zen.
With the Drunken Sage of Lake and Stream
And the Graduate of Sunset Sky,
We've laughed and talked and ascertained
Just whom the state should dignify.[5]
Loitering,
For two score years here I've remained—
In the perfect place to criticize
The coolness of a breeze at noon,
Or add poetic luster to an evening's moon.

(Ch'iao Chi. _Liu-yao P'ien, Hsien-lü._ 575.1)

And here is one in which the composer envisions himself as the ideal Taoist framed in the perfect picture of secluded retirement:

---

[5] See _CYSC_ 580.6, where Ch'iao Chi uses the same lines. The Sage and the Graduate are the woodcutter and the fisher. See below.

不占龍頭選。不入名賢傳。時時酒聖。處處詩禪。煙霞狀元。江湖醉仙。笑談便

是編修院。留連。批風抹月四十年。

綠鬢衰。朱顏改。羞把塵容畫麟臺。故園風景依然在。三頃田。五畝宅。歸去來。

門前好山雲占了。盡日無人到。松風響翠濤。槲葉燒丹灶。先生醉眠春自老。

Spring Sleep among the Hills

Marauding clouds infiltrate
The handsome hills outside his gate;
Throughout the livelong day
No passer-by will come this way.
While surfing pinetrees sound their blue-
    green sigh,
And oak leaves heat his alembic,
A drunken Taoist sleeps
And lets the aging spring go by.

(Chang K'o-chiu. *Ch'ing-chiang Yin.* 791.1)

The next four songs, I believe, were composed
in preparation for, during, or after some retirement
banquet at which each of the guests was required to
create a song on the subject of retreat and with-
drawal. It was to be done to the tune of *Ssu-k'uai Yü*,
with the additional stricture, apparently, that it in-
clude allusions—not visible in translation—to T'ao
Ch'ien (the most poetically famous retiree of all) and
end with *kuei-ch'ü-lai* "return!" This phrase from one
of T'ao Ch'ien's most famous verses had taken on
special significance by Yuan times and was always
construed to imply return to the Tao:

Retreat to Tranquillity

My once-black hair so shot with gray,
Red cheeks of youth so lined today,
A portrait of me would bring nought but
    shame
If hung in the Unicorn Hall of Fame.
But from my garden can still be discerned
The same old view—

My field of three acres,
My house with five *mu*—
I have returned.

(Ma Chih-yüan. 233.2)

Green waters, blue hills surround
A tiny hut, two acres of fertile ground.
My idleness has proven that
At last the Red Dust is spurned.[6]
Purple crabs grow fat,
Yellow chrysanthemums have bloomed,
I have returned.

(Ma Chih-yüan. 233.3)

Blue bamboo, green pines surround
Two huts of bamboo shadow and pinetree
    sound.
Happy the peace my idleness has earned!
My three paths raked,
My five willows pruned;
I have returned.

(Ma Chih-yüan. 233.4)

A jug of new wine besought,
A fresh fish new bought,
And mine eye has looked its fill
On clouds and hill—
Held as though caught

---

[6] "Red dust" is a stock term for what we designate the "rat race."

濟才。歸去來。

酒旋沽。魚新買。滿眼雲山畫圖開。清風明月還詩債。本是箇懶散人。又無甚經

翠竹邊。青松側。竹影松聲兩茅齋。太平幸得閑身在。三徑修。五柳栽。歸去來。

綠水邊。青山側。二頃良田一區宅。閑身跳出紅塵外。紫蟹肥。黃菊開。歸去來。

功
名
壯
年
今
皓
首
。
揀
得
溪
山
秀
。
清
霜
紫
蟹
肥
。
細
雨
黃
花
瘦
。
床
頭
一
壺
新
糯
酒
。

On a landscape scroll.
The breeze, the moon will repay me in verse.
I was ever a lazy soul;
How to hold a post I never learned . . .
But I've returned!

(Ma Chih-yüan. 234.1)

Though I can only speculate that the four songs above were part of a retirement party, there are, in fact, a number of very similar compositions with brief prefaces explicitly stating that they were composed for the retirement banquet of so-and-so. The Mr. Chang Tzu-chien toasted below would be entirely unknown to history had it not been for the fact that a retirement party was given for him to which the famous and prolific composer Chang K'o-chiu was invited. There must, of course, have been other guests as well, and without doubt all were expected to compose congratulatory verses celebrating Chang Tzu-chien's retirement from the post of Assistant Transport Commissioner.

*For the Retirement Banquet of Assistant Transport
Commissioner Chang Tzu-chien*

Fame flourished in your youthful career
As does white hair this retirement year.
Choose now the beauties of mountain and
     stream —
Where light frost ensures
That the purple crab matures,
And "misty rains on the thinning
     chrysanthemums."

And let your bedside jug be filled
With the best new wine there distilled!

(Chang K'o-chiu. *Ch'ing-chiang Yin.* 929.1)

Go thou, go.
To the Tao return again.
The chrysanthemums, the evergreens remain.
By draining his fated cup while he was still
  alive,
Ten centuries did his name survive.
To us, Han Hsin is not so great
As P'eng-tse's sometime magistrate.[7]

(929.2)

Withdraw to cloudy peaks:
There, happy in your own secluded den,
In harmonizing verse repeat
All lines written by T'ao Ch'ien.
May your local brew be honey-sweet,
Nearby, let fist-sized mountain chestnuts
  thrive.
Outside your window let cold-plums bloom
While crackling pine-boughs heat your room.

(929.3)

This trio of compositions, though not long on po-
etic value, shows clearly how such songs were used

去來去來歸去來。菊老青松在。生前酒一杯。死後名千載。淮陰侯不如彭澤宰。

雲巖隱居安樂窩。盡把陶詩和。村醪蜜樣甜。山栗拳來大。梅窗一爐松葉火。

---

[7] Han Hsin, Count Huai-yin, was a power in the Han court until he fell from grace. P'eng-tse was the district in which T'ao Ch'ien was, briefly, the magistrate.

去利
。名
無
。宦
情
疏
。彭
澤
升
半
微
官
祿
。蠹
魚
食
殘
架
上
書
。曉
霜
荒
盡
籬
邊
菊
。罷
官
歸

socially and what their special charms were during such occasions.

And finally, a kind of tongue-in-cheek "Joys": this one seems less eager anticipation than "everything else is fouled up, I might as well quit"! The tendency to burlesque subject matter that had become hackneyed by over-popularity is one of the charms of Yuan dynasty songs:

Idle Pleasures

Since wealth and fame eluded me
And I've no love for bureaucracy—
Even T'ao Ch'ien earned more than I—
And what books I had the silverfish ate,
And dawnfrost has made my flowers die,
I've quit my job to rusticate!

(Wu Hung-tao. *Po Pu-tuan.* 734.2)

Verses for Special Occasions

As was always the case with Chinese verse, little triumphs, small personal celebrations, or just particularly wonderful days were customarily captured in verse. Ah-li Hsi-ying's two "Lazy Cloud" songs (and one other unrelated piece of verse) are all we have attributed to that well-known non-Chinese musician—although he was a member of a coterie of famous composers, including Kuan Yün-shih, Ch'iao Chi, Wei Li-chung, and Wu Hsi-yi, all of whom wrote songs "matching" his happy little verses of guileless delight in his new studio:

Nest of the Lazy Cloud

Oh, Lazy Cloud's Nest:
When sober we drink to poetry;
Drunk, we sing our melody.
When inlaid lute has ceased to please
We set aside our books and rest,
And found no dream-built dynasties.
Completely happy with idleness,
Our days and months go shuttling past;
Wealth and honor never last,
They bloom, they fall as flowers do.
But should young spring pass joyless by,
Does not blame lie
Alone with you?

(*Tien-ch'ien Huan.* 339.1)

懶雲窩。醒時詩酒醉時歌。瑤琴不理拋書臥。無夢難柯。得清閑儘快活。日月似攛梭過。富貴比花開落。青春去也。不樂如何。

Nest of the Lazy Cloud

[Composer's preface:] Hsi-ying had a residence called Nest of the Lazy Cloud. He used this *ch'ü-p'ai* to sing of it and himself.

Oh, Nest of Lazy Cloud,
What can we offer the arriving guest?
All *we* do at Lazy Cloud
Is fall asleep still fully dressed.
Or, absorbed in idle languor live
And wonder what more life could give.
The noble find me lacking pride,
The rich think I'm too satisfied.
Ha, ha, they laugh at me, but then
Ha, ha I laugh right back again!

(*Tien-ch'ien Huan.* 339.3)

懶雲窩。客至待如何。懶雲窩裏和衣臥。儘自婆娑。想人生待則麼。貴比我高些箇。富比我恁些箇。呵呵笑我。我笑呵呵。

懶雲窩。雲窩客至欲如何。懶雲窩裏和雲臥。打會磨跎。想人生待怎麼。貴比我爭些大。富比我爭些箇。呵呵笑我。我笑呵呵。

[Composer's preface:] (Ah) Li Hsi-ying took the sobriquet Proprietor of the Nest of the Lazy Cloud to express himself. Here is a matching verse *(ho)* I made for him.

Oh, Nest of Lazy Cloud—
What can this cloudy nest
Offer to the coming guest?
That in the Lazy Cloud
He can with other clouds find rest,
And in idle leisure live,
Asking, "What do we lack that life can give?"
Saying, "The noble are not more so than I;
What have the rich that I would buy?"
Ha, ha, they laugh at us, but then,
We laugh ha, ha right back again!

(Ch'iao Chi. *Tien-ch'ien Huan.* 630.5)

The exchange involving the name of Ah-li Hsi-ying's studio appears to have been part of a fairly jolly and possibly bibulous social occasion—a most common note for songs from Xanadu to strike. But more intimate and private events are memorialized by using this form, though less frequently than in *shih*-poetry, for instance. Chapter 3 of *Songs* was devoted to compositions by Chang Yang-hao, who is probably the best-known composer of personal songs in the age of Xanadu, though certainly not the only one. "Revisiting the Waterfall," by Ch'iao Chi, already treated technically in the Introduction (page 19), is a beautiful example of a song used to celebrate a highly personal, unshared experience. On the other hand, the songs below appear to be charming commemorations of *shared* minor events (important because they are both ephemeral and highly personal), making me wish we had a tradition as strong as the Chinese of writing poetry to one another:

To the Harvest Moon—Being without Wine

The icy wheel is riding high,
The Silver River slants the sky.
An artist's hand might recreate
That vast, cold Moon-Palace gate;
I greet this glorious light above
With a flood of unleashed love.
Good friends, frank talk—the night is over
    soon.
Come, loving Goddess of the Moon,
Join us in our drink and song—
The words?
I know them not.
The wine
I stupidly forgot!

(T'ang Shih. *Shan-p'o Yang*. 1604.1)

Plum Blossoms

The finest blooms had opened to the rain
When you, my friend-beyond-the-clouds,
    arrived again.
No amount of deep-felt verse
Can ransom all those years apart,
Yet our greeting moment opened wide the
    heart.
The little kiosk and belvedere,
The zig-zag balustrade—

冰輪高駕。銀河斜掛。廣寒宮闕堪圖畫。對光華。恣歡洽。故人一夜團圓話。多

情素娥吟笑。咱。詩也。懵撒。酒也懵撒。

好花多向雨中開。佳客新從雲外來。清詩未了年前債。相逢且放懷。曲闌干碾玉

亭臺。小樹紛蝶翅。蒼苔點鹿胎。踏碎青鞋。

White as though with powdered jade.
Fanning through small trees,
Scattered butterfly-wings that blow
Fawn-dapple down below the moss-green sod,
To be broken where blue slippers trod.

(Chang K'o-chiu. *Shui-hsien tzu.* 853.2)

There is a well-known Chinese *tui-chü* (parallel couplet) expressing the finest things you can wish another: "May the loveliest flowers await your coming ere they fall / May your dearest friends arrive before you call." Chang K'o-chiu has made me believe that just such a heart-warming occasion transpired, and he signalized it with a song to give his friend-beyond-the-clouds. Further, since history-as-it-should-have-been is the only satisfactory kind, his friend soon sent back a reply written to the same matrix!

Obviously, not all personal occasions were so sanguine, and in a society whose literate and literary bureaucracy was constantly being dispatched to distant and often uncongenial posts, somber verse in the wee hours was to be expected. Sometimes these men chose the song form to express their loneliness, as in the following:

Chekiang autumn, Wu-shan night.
My spirits ebb as the neap-tide flows;
As hills mass in the distance,
So my resentment grows.
Geese from the border forts are here;
Summer hibiscus, already sere.

浙江秋。吳山夜。愁隨潮去。恨與山疊。塞雁來。芙蓉謝。冷雨青燈讀書舍。待

離別怎忍離別。今宵醉也。明朝去也。寧奈些些。

Cold rain outside the study,
Uncertain lamp within.
Waiting to go; hating to go
I'll stay drunk tonight—
Tomorrow, first light
Must see my journey begin.
I shall endure, therefore,
Yet a little more.

(Yao Sui. *P'u-tien Lo.* 209.2)

Or to convey general depression over the progress
of their careers:

Feelings on Returning

My writings, lacking lofty tone,
Won me no service near the throne.
My family, sprung from common men,
Barred me from the Han-lin Yüan.
Seek fame in distant lands who dares—
I feared their dank mephitic airs.
Now that hard old age has come
I long to see my childhood home—
Nor can I disregard
My journey's dreams and griefs
That left a soul thus scarred.
On Stone-man Range the storm clouds throng,
Waves disturb the Yang-tzu Chiang—
The river's wide, the mountain's long.

(Chang K'o-chiu. *Shui Hsien-tzu.* 857.2)

淡文章不到紫薇郎。小根腳難登白玉堂。遠功名卻怕黃茅瘴。老來也思故鄉。想途中夢感魂傷。雲莽莽馮公嶺。浪淘淘揚子江。水遠山長。

The Fisherman

As I have mentioned elsewhere in this book, there was one trade, fishing, which appealed greatly to poets and painters.[8] In large part, it must be admitted, this was so precisely because none of these educated and artistic gentlemen ever had firsthand experience earning a livelihood capturing something so unpredictable as fish: in some respects fishing is more maddeningly at the mercy of weather and season than is farming. The negative aspects of the trade were lost on the poet, to whom the picturesque fisherman and his ways had a powerful appeal—primarily, I imagine, because of the fisher's hardy independence and self-sufficiency: he had but to moor the vehicle of his trade to turn it instantly into his dwelling, and the very lakes and rivers he traveled— the "ten-thousand hectares of shining glass"—supplied all his needs. The fisherman was completely mobile in a society almost insanely preoccupied with a person's place of registration and the propriety of remaining there. This kind of freedom certainly attracted the intelligentry, who were only too conversant with the trammels of societal and governmental interference (they were its representatives, after all):

---

[8] The popularity of the fisherman as subject matter for Yuan songs is made clear in a curious set of twenty compositions by Ch'iao Chi (*CYSC*, pp. 579–82) under the title "Songs of the Fisherman," each of the twenty written to a different rhyme. Ch'iao probably chose the fisher for his twenty pieces because he knew his audience accepted the fisherman quite readily as a song topic, and because he knew he would have numerous well-worn phrases and images ready-made, since nearly all his contemporaries had also written songs on the subject.

The Fisherman

Sunset colors river and sky . . .
At Wildford his boat is beached,
His nets spread on the bar to dry.
No child, no parent is prey to care—
Their easy chatter fills the air.
He has thick new wine, lotus root
With orange sweet,
Scaly fish, purple crab, pink shrimp to eat.
And with his bowl and cup drained dry,
Throughout the night he'll lie
Content and drunk
Amid reed-flowers where the moon has sunk.

(Chao Hsien-hung. *Man-t'ing Fang.* 1179.2)

Here, as in so many songs, the fisher and his entire
family are at home in their night mooring: the river
has supplied everything they need save the wine
which—numerous songs testify—is to be gotten by
trading a few fish.

There is also ample evidence from surviving
paintings that the fisherman and his ways were a
favored subject for graphic as well as literary artists:

Evening in the Fishing Village

The "sounding sticks" are silent now,[9]
Sunset shadows stretching long.
From willowdyke, snatches of the fishers'
 song.
Spread on cottagers' wicker fences,
Drying nets hang down—

鳴榔罷。閃暮光。綠楊隄數聲魚唱。掛柴門幾家閑曬網。都撮在捕魚圖上。

錦鱗魚紫蟹。紅蝦。杯盤罷。爭些醉煞。和月宿蘆花。

江天晚霞。舟橫野渡。網曬汀沙。一家老幼無牽掛。恣意喧譁。新糯酒香橙藕芽。

(The Cleveland Museum of Art, The Severance and Greta Millikin Purchase Fund)

All caught in this painting
Of a little fishing town.

(Ma Chih-yüan. *Lo-mei Feng*. 246.2)

[variorum]

Upstream of the setting sun
Where the Oldford Shallows run
Lie fishers' huts—two or three
Scattered randomly.
Fishing boats moored on the strand,
Grouped like fingers of a hand,
And sun-dried nets hanging down—
Caught in this painting of a fishing town.

(246.2n)

In addition to being the embodiment of simple and idyllic freedom, the fisherman and his woodcutter companion are part of a curious allusion occurring with great frequency in songs from Xanadu.[10] When, in the lyrics of popular songs, these two free spirits "chatted with one another" or "told each other tales," the Yuan dynasty audience knew the implied subject of their colloquy would be the vanity of past dynastic glories. It is aimost a certainty that the phrase "woodsman and fisher's idle chatter" and its association with *sic transit gloria* come originally

夕陽外。古渡傍。兩三家不成圈巷。一簇兒聚船人曬網。都撮在捕魚圖上。

---

[9] Clubs beaten against the boat to drive fish into the nets. Note the auditory components of this painting.

[10] In *Songs* (pp. 96–105), I noted over twenty-five songs containing some version of it.

from a very popular Sung lyric (tz'u) composed by Chang Sheng (992–1077):

> How many of the Six Dynasties
> Here rose and here fell?
> All are now but *idle tales*
> *That woodsmen and fishers tell.*
> Beside the looming ruin I rest
> Downcast, watching a sun gone cold,
> Slip wordlessly west.

多少六朝興廢事。盡入漁樵閑話。悵望倚層樓。寒日無言西下。

Yuan dynasty song-writers habitually incorporated phrases or lines from other poetry into their popular songs, and the more widely used the cliché, the better the songsmiths liked it. Popular entertainment, one must remember, depends more heavily on familiarity than originality.

But the story does not end there. Where the original context of the allusion merely implies that the sight of ancient ruins (presumably easily visible to the woodsman and fisher as they ply their trades) provoked their leisurely chats about the past, in the song-set below (and in many other Yüan songs, long and short) their idle interest in these traces of bygone days has been extended to include reading and criticizing texts (an unlikely pursuit for fishers and woodsmen) which dealt with these vanished former glories:

Fisherman's Joys

Tuan-cheng Hao
A fishing skiff with small mat roof
Against the chill and wave.

釣艇小苫寒波。蓑笠軟遮風雨。打魚人活計蕭疏。儂家鸚鵡洲邊住。對江景眞堪趣。黃蘆岸似錦舖。白蘋渡如雪糢。野鷗閑自來。自去。暮雲閑或轉。或舒。日已無。月漸出。映蟾光滿川修竹。助風聲兩岸黃蘆。收綸罷釣尋歸路。酒美魚鮮樂

Rush cloak with arum hat, pliant proof
Against the wind and rain.
Your fisher's livelihood is frugal, plain,
But you live your life on Parrot Isle
And glory in its river scenes the while.

Kun Hsiu-ch'iu
Your yellow reed-embroidered shores.
Your whiteweed at the ford,
A misty mound of summer snow.
As they will, the wild gulls come and go
While idle evening cloud-banks build and grow.
When the sun is set
The moontoad comes in view;
Its slow light floods the stream
With shadowy bamboo.
The rustle of shore rushes
Fills the wind.
Nets in, rods secure,
Heading home to moor.
There to eat
Your fish fresh-caught and wine that's sweet—
Pleasure upon pleasure,
Whose joys are so complete?

T'ang Hsiu-ts'ai
Tether for sleep your little boat.
Waken when you float
In rush-bloom shallows—
Drifting, bobbing, unrestrained.
All the night you have remained
Far from courts and market-places.
Gone are once familiar faces:
The woodsman's now your only friend.

恰所有
離拘餘
了。。
聚市此
野朝樂
猿遠誰
白。如
雲故。
洞人睡
口疏時
。。節
早有把
來樵肩
到夫舟
散做來
清伴纜
風侶住
。。。
綠雨覺
陰才來
深過也
處山又
。色流
模在
相糊蘆
逢。花
的月淺
伴初處
侶升。
。桂蕩
豈影蕩
問扶悠
箇疏悠
賢。無
愚
。

T'o Pu-shan
After a passing rain,
The mountain mists remain.
On one, then another the risen moon gave
Shadows to the cassia trees,
Light to Gibbon Grotto at White-Cloud Cave,
Then, green, deep, hidden, shone
On the Place of Cooling Breeze.

Tsui T'ai-p'ing
Well-met friends will never weigh
Which of them is dull or wise.
Woodsman and fisher, men laugh and say,
Discuss the past and judge today.
With open hearts you criticize
The merits of some poem's line.
Forgetting cares with cups of wine,
Idly angling when you please—
Both of you content, at ease.

Wei-sheng
The woodsman leaves for his hills again;
Here by the river I remain.
Another day we two will meet—
Spiced wine to sup and fish to eat.
We'll read from history books and walk,
Debating as we stroll along.
Step by step we'll settle with our talk
Whose deeds were right and whose were
　　wrong.

(Chang K'o-chiu. *Tuan-cheng Hao lien-t'ao.* 987.1)

人間開口笑樵漁。會談今論古。放懷講會詩中句。忘憂飲會杯中趣。清閑釣會水

中魚。俺兩箇心足來意足。樵夫別我山中去。我離樵夫水上居。來日相逢共一

處。旋取香醪旋打魚。散誕逍遙看古書。問甚麼誰是誰非。俺兩箇慢慢的數。

從
別
後
。
音
信
絕
。
薄
情
種
害
煞
人
也
。
逢
一
箇
見
一
箇
因
話
說
。
不
信
你
耳
輪
兒
不
熱
。

In some songs from Xanadu the woodcutter and fisher are referred to as "unlettered statesmen," as "the drunken sages of lake and stream," and "graduates of sunset skies," but in the song above their learning is not vaguely alluded to with fair phrase or poetic reference—the two of them read the poetry and ancient books and delight one another with their criticism. I believe this poetic metamorphosis of two humble (but appealing) tradesmen into rustic scholars also comes about in songs from Xanadu because of the popularity of Chang Sheng's lines.

Proverbial Wisdom and Cautionary Songs

Since most Chinese proverbs have a distinctive form— a pair of rhyming four syllable lines—and since the four-beat line was one of the common features of songs from Xanadu, it stood to reason that sooner or later the former would be incorporated into the latter. Fragments of proverbs are to be found scattered everywhere throughout the songs, but the next two actually convert omen-proverbs into songs:

> You left
> And there's been
> No word since.
> One can die from a lover's indifference!
> Everyone I meet,
> Everyone I see,
> I tell them what was done to me—
> If your ears aren't burning, they ought to be!

(Ma Chih-yüan. *Lo-mei Feng.* 247.6)

You left me
And I've not heard
Since that time a single word—
Though once, in a dream, you came to me.
From everyone who passes through
I seek what they might know of you—
If your eyes aren't twitching, they ought to be!

(Ma Chih-yüan. *Lo-mei Feng.* 247.7)

The burden of the first of these greatly resembles our English, "My ears are burning, someone's speaking of me"; the second proverb seems not to be common in China today: twitching of the left or right eye means, in some traditions, good or evil in the offing. We have no counterpart for it in English, though "right palm itches—money coming in; left palm itches—money going out" is somewhat similar.

Given that the metrical requirements of songs from Xanadu in many places matched those commonly used by proverbs, and that song writers habitually mitered into their compositions well-known lines from older verse (especially those from homiletic hornbooks and collections of "popular parlor poetry"), the cautionary song, the singable sermon, was frequently in evidence. Below is one of the cleverer examples.

Sigh over the World

Quests for hollow fame
Forever disavow.
Nor ever let a crafty scheme
Grind furrows in your brow.
All your livelong life forswear

從別後。音信杳。夢兒裏也曾來到。問人知行到一萬遭。不信你眼皮兒不跳。

虛名休就。眉頭休皺。終身更不遭機彀。抱官囚。為誰愁。功名半紙難能夠。爭

如漆園蝶夢叟。常。緊閉口。閑。且袖手。

殘
花
醞
釀
蜂
兒
蜜
。
細
雨
調
和
燕
子
泥
。
綠
窗
春
睡
覺
來
遲
。
誰
喚
起
。
窗
外
曉
鶯
啼
。

The governmental snare—
For once you've run afoul the law
Who'll be left to care?
Is a half a sheet of merit such a prize?
I'd rather be, contrariwise,
The elder of Chi-garden
Who dreamed his butterflies.
Dictum:
Keep mum!
If you perceive
Your hands are idle,
Shove them up your sleeve!

(Tseng Jui. *Shan-p'o Yang.* 493.4)

And, finally, as is the case with all poetic traditions I know, the vernal season either inspires or furnishes the background for more songs from Xanadu than all other topics—with the possible exception of love, with which it is closely conjoined. Below, as a coda (*wei-sheng*) for this chapter, one example to stand for hundreds:

Springscene

Over-ripe blossoms brew honey for the bee.
Misty rains soften earth for swallow masonry.
My spring windows green a-pace
My spring slumberings grow long.
Who calls me now . . . ?
Orioles singing their firstlight song.

(Hu Ch'i-yü. *Yang-ch'un Ch'ü.* 68.1)

4

Snowy Day near Xanadu: Feng Tzu-chen and His Songs

> *Poetry is the spontaneous overflow of power-*
> *ful feelings: it takes its origin from emotion*
> *recollected in tranquillity.*

Wordsworth

"In the year 1302 I was in Shang-ching with the Peking entertainer Yü-yüan Hsiu and her troupe, waiting out a snowstorm," writes Feng Tzu-chen in his introduction to the most remarkable group of compositions from Xanadu. "These ladies," he goes on,

> regretted that no one had ever done "continu-ations" to Po Wu-chiu's [Po Pen's] "Parrot Island Song" *[Ying-wu Ch'ü].* "The literati we know," they went on, "were constrained in doing so by the

extraordinary demands of its prosody" . . . The gen-
tlemen then raised their cups and challenged me to
compose matches for it, taking as my subject matter
the scenery of Pien-wu, Shang-tu, and T'ien-ching.

Following this introduction come *forty-two* "continu-
ations" to the song by Po Pen!

History is completely silent about this junket to
what must have been the Khan's summer capital,
but it was an old imperial prerogative peremptorily
to summon entertainment troupes to perform at the
palace—and, of course, middle-rank officialdom
was always on tap whenever the Son of Heaven
called. It must have been rather late in the season for
a khan to be in residence at Shang-tu (Xanadu), as
witness the snowstorm.[1] It appears he had sum-
moned Feng Tzu-chen, a Peking entertainment
troupe, and assorted "gentlemen" (scholar-bureau-
crats) to attend him. They were all making their way
back to Peking, and had not got very far, when the
snowstorm overtook them to become the occasion
for Feng's Forty-Two Variations.

Since we seldom possess any information on
circumstances surrounding the composition of Yuan
dynasty songs, his short but quite edifying preface
is of great interest—if only because of its singularity.
Its implications will be examined shortly, but let me
here recount something of the forty-two pieces this
unusual poet (he referred to himself as "The Wierd
Taoist") introduces with his preface.

---

[1] Marco Polo tells us that Kublai used regularly to leave Shang-tu
"on the twenty-eighth of the August moon."

When the gentlemen in Feng's party challenged him to *match* Po's song, they used the term *ho*. A Chinese poet was frequently required to *ho* a drinking companion's piece, or he might, as a sign of respect, match some or all of the verse of an admired *former* poet of the past. In either case he would traditionally use the same matrix, compatible subject matter and phraseology, and the same rhyme *class* as the original. Feng's forty-two matching songs, however, use not merely the same rhyming sounds as Po's "Parrot Island Song," but exactly the *same rhyming characters*.[2] Furthermore, if we are to believe Feng's preface (later we will examine why, perhaps, we should not), the implication cannot be avoided that in response to the challenge he proceeded to compose forty-two "continuations" on the spot.

This tour de force in the hands of a lesser poet could have amounted to little more than forty-two clever anagrams, but in fact the group contains a remarkable number of beautiful songs, and there is no reason why Feng should not have preened himself on them—whether he wrote them extempore or at his leisure afterwards. Though legend has it that Feng did forthwith dash the preface off along with all forty-two songs, a moment's reflection makes it clear that in truth the preface had to have been written after the fact—at some later time when he was recalling the event.

Now, I do not doubt that Feng did compose some pieces impromptu on the occasion of the snowstorm, nor do I question whether such an elegant

---

[2] *Pu-yün* or *tzu-yün*.

and literary group—we are justified in imagining it to have been such—would journey equipped with inkstone, brush, and paper. I confess difficulty, however, picturing such an aggregation, whose members must have been quite used to occupying center-stage themselves, sitting about waiting for the snow to stop or Feng to complete all of his forty-two songs (whichever came first), though the legend implies that they did. It also abuses common sense to imagine a dedicated scribbler like Feng writing a preface after the event and not adding more songs to those he wrote during the snowstorm, thereby bringing the aggregate up to its impressive total.

The little we know of Feng Tzu-chen is all of a piece with the legend of the forty-two variations on one snowy day. Everything contributes to the picture of him as an eccentric literatus and a talented musician. As evidence for the former, this "traveller from Atlantis" as he also called himself, is elsewhere characterized as one who

> would frequently go to his desk, after having stationed three attendants nearby with wetted brushes, and begin furiously to write. However much paper there happened to be, he would fill it all up in a trice. His subject matter was always rich as strong wines and his style was like a crowded brocade.

Or again:

> Feng was known to the age for his wide learning and lofty style. When he was somewhat taken with drink, his ears would grow hot and his heroic spirit would soar . . . in a single effort he could compose pieces of not less than a thousand and often as many as ten-thousand words . . . in truth, a paragon of the times.[3]

His contemporary, the talented Uigur Kuan Yün-shih, called Feng's style "pungent and luminous."

The only evidence we need of his musicality is that he undoubtedly did compose a number of songs on the spot for the most demanding and knowledgeable audience imaginable—a troupe of professional singers from the capital. He writes in his preface that, regarding his model, they warned him:

> "The rhyme in the second line creates difficulties for the whole composition, and the first and sixth syllables of the last line have to be falling and low-rising tones respectively to have the prosody come out right. Furthermore, if the composition be not done thus, it will be impossible to sing."

Despite these admonitions, Feng was confident enough to dash off songs which, we must suppose, satisfied his peers poetically and the ladies musically.

Feng Tzu-chen held a mid-level post in the government, and it could be expected that someone in his position and with his proclivities would have left more songs for posterity.[4] However, as is so often the case, accident decreed otherwise. It appears that the somewhat extravagant conditions under which, legend tells us, the Forty-Two Variations were composed served to make them attractive for later anthologies in which they were ultimately preserved, yet all save two other short songs by Feng have vanished.[5]

---

[3] Both anecdotes are repeated in *CYSC*.

[4] Many verses from his collection of *shih*-poetry do appear in *Yüan-shih Hsüan*.

[5] Anecdote has it that he once wrote a verse to the matrix *Che-ku*

However, let us now consider the words Feng puts into the mouths of the ladies. He has them remark that no one they knew could do a satisfactory continuation to Po Pen's song. He spells out for us (through their lips) the musical and metrical difficulties, and then proceeds to wow the brilliant gentlemen and elegant ladies of the gathering (not to mention future readers) with forty-two examples! Feng would not have been the first writer modestly to report the words of third parties in such a fashion that they cast the best light on something he himself had done. We must be intrigued to discover, therefore, that despite what Feng has his ladies contend, Wang Yün (1227–1304), Lu Chin (*chin-shih* degree 1268), and Liu Ming-chung (1243–1318)—all of whom were senior to Feng—not only wrote "continuations" but composed them (as Feng had) using the same rhyming characters as the original. Now, we could become Feng partisans and maintain that the ladies might not have *known* these men—though they were among the most famous song writers of their era—or that the ladies felt the continuations by them were not satisfactory, but a simpler explanation occurs to me: some time after he had been on that high-fashion junket, Feng wrote a preamble leaving out a few facts, leaving in a few implications, and making an altogether better story out of the incident. What's wrong with that?

T'ien dedicated to the famous entertainer Chu-lien Hsiu. It is no longer extant. See chapter 1.

The snowy journey also served to add luster to Po Pen's name as a composer of *ch'ü;* apart from the one song, General Po was far better known as a painter and writer of *shih* poetry. In *CYSC* (p. 447) the editor remarks that "Po's 'Parrot Island Song' was extremely famous, since later there were numerous continuations *(ho)* made for it." From our modern perspective, unable as we are to guess at six-hundred-year-old nuances of taste, his composition does not seem exceptional, but it is worth reproducing here simply to let the reader see what we're talking about:

Parrot Island Song

I dwell on Parrot Island where I can
Be an unlettered fisherman.
I can float
Safe among the flowering whitecaps
In my shallow boat,
And soundly sleep
Through Chiang-nan's smoking rain.

(yao)[6]
Then, when I awake again
Green hills fill my eye.
I shake my cape of rushes dry
And sail back home.
I used to curse Old Heaven—
It was he
Who put me where I am.

---

[6] A repeat of the melody using different words.

農家鸚鵡洲邊住。是箇不識字漁父。浪花中一葉扁舟。睡煞江南煙雨。

覺來時滿眼青山。抖擻綠蓑歸去。算從前錯怨天公。甚也有安排我處。

Now I see
Heaven *made* this special place for me.

(*Hei-ch'i Nu.* 447.1)

Personally, I prefer some of Feng's "matches" to
the original, but if imitation is to be the test of repu-
tation, Feng's contributions to Po's fame must out-
weigh all others. However, what of those matching
songs written earlier than Feng's? Wang Yün's piece
"Visiting Chin-shan Temple" (96.2), for example, is
the earliest *Hei-ch'i Nu* composition to indicate inspi-
ration from "Parrot Island Song." Its preface says, in
part,

> *Hei-ch'i Nu* was being used as a toasting song when
> Secretary Chung-hsien said to me, "The verses are
> pleasant enough, but the name of the song matrix
> *Hei-ch'i Nu* [Black-lacquered Crossbow] appears to
> me to lack elegance. Don't you think we should refer
> to it as "Chiang-nan's Smoking Rain?"

Since the Secretary's suggested title for the matrix
consists of the last four characters from a line of
"Parrot Island Song," there can be no doubt that Po's
composition was much on their minds, even though
they may not actually have been trying to "match"
it.

It is also interesting to note that the matching in
this complex of compositions is not limited to Po's
song: Chang K'o-chiu's (fl. 1317) first "match"
claims in its title to be "using Feng's rhymes." Ex-
actly what Chang means by this is hardly clear since
all of the rhyming characters in his version of the
Hei-ch'i Nu differ from those in Feng's forty-two
continuations! Chang's second "match" is entitled

"Parting from Friends at High-Sands, Using 'Parrot Island' Rhymes," and in the latter song he uses all of Po's (and, of course, Feng's) rhyming characters save the last, where *ch'u* "to come out" is used instead of *ch'u* "place." It is not entirely apparent, therefore, what Chang's second title meant either. But one implication is unmistakable from both these songs; Chang K'o-chiu, the most prolific composer of a generation older than Feng Tzu-chen, knows both the original and, it appears, Feng's by-then famous matches for it.

To complete this group of "continuations," there are two songs (*CYSC* 1154.1,2) by Lü Chi-min (about whom we know nothing at all) titled "Sent to a Friend"; below the title in smaller type are the words "using his rhymes." Lü's rhyming characters are identical with the original "Parrot Island" (as are Feng's, of course) so there is no way to be certain whether "friend" refers to Po or Feng, though I believe it to have been the latter.

The reader may object that earlier on I displayed unwonted skepticism about Feng's version of what transpired that snowy day near Xanadu when he entertained traveling companions with his compositions. I have not meant to be unfair, but simply recognize in Feng a personality more interested in a good story than the literal truth. As one other indication of Feng's propensity to broad interpretations, let me offer the following: You will remember that his gentlemen friends limited the allowable subject matter for Feng's *ho* to "the scenery of Pien-wu, Shang-tu, and T'ien-ching." (I admit that I know of no Pien-wu, but to fit with the other two city names, it should refer to the old Chin capital of K'ai-feng).

Now, even granting a poet can always be expected to approach any subject from a unique angle of vision, it strikes me that Feng shows more than a little indifference to the suggested restrictions in such songs as "Traveller Fishing in Lake Tung-t'ing," "Remembering Westlake," and "Early Summer on the Ch'ien-t'ang." All of these locations are far, far to the south of the areas delimited by the "gentlemen." In fact, with the exception of two verses about Yen-nan, I can find only one composition which clearly fits the northern geographical requirements. Variation 33 is titled "Arrival at the Upper Capital" and begins

> Saddles off west of the Shan
> Ended our northward trail.
> Along the ancient roads
> Never a farmer seen.[7]
> But vast flat sands, fine grass, pale green,
> Where the Chin-lien river's daily rains prevail
> . . .

Whether or not I'm right in my identification of Pien-wu,[8] consider the subject matter of some of Feng's other variations: "Brief Dream of Glory," "On Quitting the Capital," "The Lan-t'ing Handscroll," "Portrait of P'ang and the Hermit," "Sentiments," "Handscroll Showing Chu Mai-ch'en Bearing Faggots," and "On a Screen Depicting the *Four Hoary-*

---

[7] Meaning only herdsmen were in evidence.

[8] Tseng Yung-yi believes it means "Pien-liang *and* the Wu district."

Heads." None of this second group is concerned except in the most tangential fashion with scenery of any kind.

Since the true enterprise for poets is good poetry, no matter what formal strictures they may choose to adopt or ignore, I am certain the fair-minded reader will agree that the least important qualification for any composer would be the ability or willingness to observe the rules of some inconsequential literary diversion. I hope the selections below, translated from Feng's Forty-Two Variations, will convince this same reader that wherever, whenever, and under whatever rules Feng wrote them, they are good poetry, "pungent and luminous," as Kuan Yün-shih put it.

The first four variations employ the kind of landscape-artists' technique that takes for granted viewers' involvement in the scenery and challenges them to focus on a human figure in the composition that gives proportion to the totality of the painting. In each successive song below, concentration on the human figures grows, until by the fourth, what little scenery remains is all confined within the hunchback's fenced garden.

A Peasant Thirsts for Rain

Year in, year out
Behind the ox the farmer grips his plough;
Yet the last few days have brought about
A troubled, furrowed brow.
(Rice shoots now are grown so stout
They fairly burst their blossoms forth.)
Oh, how they thirst, farmer and grain,
For darkling sky, for thunder and rain.

年年牛背扶犂住。近日最懊惱殺農父。稻苗肥恰待抽花。渴煞青天雷雨。

霞不近人情。截斷玉虹南去。望人間三尺甘霖。看一片閑雲起處。

恨殘

孤村三兩人家住。終日對野叟田父。説今朝綠水平橋。昨日溪南新雨。碧天邊

雲歸巖穴。白鷺一行飛去。便芒鞋竹杖行春。問底是青帘舞處。

(yao)

He curses colored wisps in the evening sky—
They'll never satisfy
His human wish.
He hates the half formed arcs-of-jade
That southward fade.
Nor can that single, idle cloud sustain
His hopes for sweet and drenching rain.

(342.1)

Clearing Skies at Wildford

Lonely village:
Two, three families live this way.
I talk with a gleaner, a farmer the livelong day;
This morning green water rose
High as the bridge's beam
From yesterday's downpour, south of their
     stream.

(yao)

Now, slipping into gorges that notch the ridge,
Clouds just rim blue sky.
White egrets in a line wing by.
Grass sandals, bamboo staff,
Striding into spring I go!
Where does the wineshop curtain blow?

(342.4)

The Fishermen

Like fledgling egrets, in their bristling coats.
Hunched, motionless they sit
Throughout the day by Sandgull Spit—
The ancient angler and the one who reels the
　　seine.
The sun sinks, they dry their nets
And stow their poles of cane,
As a rising southwind drives before it rain.

(yao)
Abandoned on Willowdyke, far abaft
Stands their solitary mooring stake.
As white caps rise and slap their craft,
Already they think on tomorrow's dawn
When the tide is slack and the moon is gone,
When their boat is drifting near
A shoal where reed-flowers sink, then
　　reappear.

(343.1)

Old Gardener

He lives below the hill,
One hen and a hound for company.
From behind his wicker gate
The sound of laughter reaches me—
Old Humpback the gardener is tending his
　　plot.
Standing by the windlass
He sprinkles from an earthen pot
Water as rich as the unguent rains of spring.

沙鷗灘鷺襯依住。鎮日坐釣叟綸父。趁斜陽曬網收竿。又是南風催雨。

綠楊隄

忘繫孤椿。白浪打將船去。想明朝月落潮平。在掩映蘆花淺處。

柴門雞犬山前住。笑語聽傴背園父。轆轤邊抱甕澆畦。點點陽春膏雨。

菜花間

蝶也飛來。又趁暖風雙去。杏梢紅韭嫩泉香。是老瓦盆邊飲處。

山林朝市都曾住。
忠孝兩字報君父。
利名場反覆如雲。
又要商量陰雨。

便天公

有眼難開。
袖手不如家去。
更蛾眉強學時粧。
是老子平生懶處。

(yao)

From plant to flower spiraling
Flicker the butterflies.
Or, catching an eddy of warming air
They soar aloft, pair upon pair.
On his apricots the red buds swell,
All his leeks grow succulent.
From his well
Comes water with a spicy scent;
And there, from a jug of rude design
He sips this wine.

(344.2)

The final variations below do not have much in common save a faint whiff of *sic transit gloria mundi*. However, taken in conjunction with the preceding four, they do give a good picture of the latitude in subject matter Feng Tzu-chen allowed himself under the general heading of "scenery around Shang-tu."

On Quitting the Capital

I've dwelt in court and countryside;
Both king and father satisfied
By faith and filiality.
But, fickle as shifting clouds
Are the worlds of fame and gain—
Where one is always on the watch for sudden
rain.

(yao)

Heaven may have eyes, though I doubt that
    they can see.
So, better far to go back home
Than serve here helplessly,
Since I was always loath to try—
For the sake of patronage—
To paint already well-shaped brows
To conform to some new rage.

(343.2)

Short Dream of Splendor

Vermillion gates, their noble mansions empty
    now.
Rustic halls, happy with men who guide a
    plow.
Wealth and fame—barren blossoms of a
    moment,
Or leaves that fall when westwinds blow
And bring their ragged rain.

(yao)

Oh, would we were north of the river again!
In our little orchid boat we'd go
To await a cold-plum's blossoming—
Before a blighting frost but after snow—
Then singing, down the stream we'd pole
Over icy deep and shallow shoal.

(341.2)

朱
門
空
宅
無
人
住
。
村
院
快
活
煞
耕
父
。
霎
時
間
富
貴
虛
花
。
落
葉
西
風
殘
雨
。

總
不
如

水
北
相
逢
。
一
棹
木
蘭
舟
去
。
待
霜
前
雪
後
梅
開
。
傍
幾
曲
寒
潭
淺
處
。

黃金難買朱顏住。駟馬客羨跨牛父。石將軍百斛明珠。幾日歡雲娛雨。

一瞬流鶯。萬事夕陽西去。舊嬋娟落。在誰家。箇裏是高人省處。

江湖難比山林住。種果父勝刺船父。看春花又看秋花。不管顛風狂雨。

白浪滔天。我自醉歌眠去。到中流手腳忙時。則靠着柴扉深處。

趁春歸

盡人間

Sentiments

Gold coins cannot restore
The bloom of youth:
The wealthy traveler in his coach-and-four
Doth often find
Much to envy in the uncouth hind
Slouching on his ox.
General Shih used all his treasure—
Gems to fill a bushel measure—
To secure
His lovely paramour;
But how long did they play the game
Of clouds and rain?[9]

(yao)

When the season comes again
Seize all of spring;
Too soon the oriole has taken wing,
Too soon all good things are done—
Vanished like the setting sun.
Where lies the general's beauty now?
The wise man knows all things are one.

(348.3)

Sentiments II

It's hard to live on lakes and waterways;
I would rather spend my days
In hill or wood.

---

[9] Shih Ch'ung spent a fortune in jewels for his beautiful concubine, Green Pearl. His enemy saw and coveted her and captured the general. Green Pearl leaped from her pavilion to kill herself.

I would sooner be
The one who plants a fruiting tree
Than he who poles his boat.
I'd watch it blossom in the spring
And tend my flowers in the fall
Secure against the unexpected squall.

(yao)
When everywhere in the world of men,
White breakers leap
Against the sky
I just drink and sing myself to sleep.
When pressed, mid-stream, by sudden urgency,
I will rely
On my wattle hut's obscurity.

(349.1)

Idle Thoughts at Mountain Pavilion

Clever the woodsman who chose to dwell
Among the peaks atop the hill:
"Whenever an aging limb decays,
The tree is done with its flowering days—
Each twig, each leaf has suffered its fill
Of wind and rain."

(yao)
"Friends called me back to former ways;
But, better to never have left in vain
Than have to retrace your steps again."
He pointed past his gate and said
Of the mountain ranges overspread

嗟峨峰頂移家住。是箇不喞嚕樵父。爛柯時樹老無花。葉葉枝枝風雨。

喚我歸來。卻道不如休去。指門前萬疊雲山。是不費青蚨買處。

故人曾

With clouds, "What coin could buy
The scene out there which greets the eye?"

(341.1)

With these seven masterful compositions by the intriguing Feng Tzu-chen, the reader has been given what I consider a fair overview of the *ch'ü* genre—from wineshop jingle to poignant poetry.

We know so little of the music to which these words were written—and so much less about the way lyrics were supposed to have been set to it—that you and I must be content to read them as though they were literary verse, but I hope this little book has furnished enough background to help the reader keep in mind and appreciate the fact that these were once *songs* from Xanadu.

Index